★ ★ SCHOLASTIC BOOK OF ★ ★
PRESIDENTS

ALSO BY GEORGE SULLIVAN

100 Years in Photographs
Alamo!
In the Line of Fire: Eight Women War Spies
The Day Pearl Harbor Was Bombed
The Day We Walked on the Moon
The Day the Women Got the Vote
How the White House Really Works
They Shot the President: Ten True Stories
Unsolved! Famous Real Life Mysteries
Helen Keller: Her Life in Pictures
Built to Last: Building America's Amazing Bridges,
Dams, Tunnels, and Skyscrapers
Disaster! The Destruction of Our Planet

FROM THE *IN THEIR OWN WORDS* SERIES
Abraham Lincoln
Davy Crockett
Harriet Tubman
Helen Keller
Lewis and Clark
Paul Revere
Pocahontas
Thomas Edison
The Wright Brothers

SCHOLASTIC BOOK OF ★
PRESIDENTS

GEORGE SULLIVAN

SCHOLASTIC INC.

O'Dile Kory and Tim Sullivan read the manuscript copy for the recent additions to this book, correcting errors and making solid suggestions for improvement. I'm very grateful to them both.

—George Sullivan

Photos ©: cover Trump: Ida Mae Astute/ABC/Getty Images; cover, 3 White House: agaliza/iStockphoto; cover, 3 Bush head: Courtesy George W. Bush Presidential Library and Museum; cover background texture: Textures.com; cover, 3 Obama body: cherezoff/iStockphoto; cover, 3 Nixon body: GlobalStock/iStockphoto; cover, 3 Kennedy body: Aldo Murillo/iStockphoto; cover flag: spawns/iStockphoto; cover, 3 Bush body: stockyimages/Thinkstock; cover, 3 Lincoln head: Alexander Gardner/Library of Congress; cover, 3 Nixon head: Library of Congress; cover, 3 Washington head: Gilbert Stuart/Detroit Publishing Co./Library of Congress; cover, 3 Kennedy head: Library of Congress; cover, 3 Obama head: Annie Leibovitz/White House Photo; cover, 3 Lincoln's body: Library of Congress; cover, 3 Washington's body: Library of Congress; 7: Pete Souza/White House Photo; 9: Ronald Reagan Presidential Library; 10: John F. Kennedy Presidential Library and Museum; 13: Stephan Savoia/AP Images; 18: Library of Congress; 20: agaliza/iStockphoto; 21: Library of Congress; 22: Courtesy of the General Mills Archives and Jerome F. Ryan Estate; 23: Edward Savage/National Gallery of Art; 24: Library of Congress; 26: Courtesy of the General Mills Archives and Jerome F. Ryan Estate; 27: National Park Service; 29: Courtesy of the General Mills Archives and Jerome F. Ryan Estate; 30: kreicher/iStockphoto; 31: Mark Newman/Getty Images; 33: Courtesy of the General Mills Archives and Jerome F. Ryan Estate; 34: traveler1116/iStockphoto; 36: Courtesy of the General Mills Archives and Jerome F. Ryan Estate; 37: US Army Center of Military History; 39: Courtesy of the General Mills Archives and Jerome F. Ryan Estate; 40: Detroit Publishing Co./Library of Congress; 42: Courtesy of the General Mills Archives and Jerome F. Ryan Estate; 43: Library of Congress; 45: Courtesy of the General Mills Archives and Jerome F. Ryan Estate; 48: Courtesy of the General Mills Archives and Jerome F. Ryan Estate; 49: Kurz & Allison/Library of Congress; 51: Courtesy of the General Mills Archives and Jerome F. Ryan Estate; 52: Library of Congress; 53 left: Francisco Anelli/The Granger Collection; 53 right: traveler1116/iStockphoto; 54: Courtesy of the General Mills Archives and Jerome F. Ryan Estate; 55: Library of Congress/S.Dupuis/Alamy Images; 56: Frederic Remington/Library of Congress; 57: Courtesy of the General Mills Archives and Jerome F. Ryan Estate; 59: Courtesy of the General Mills Archives and Jerome F. Ryan Estate; 60: John Plumbe/Library of Congress; 62: Courtesy of the General Mills Archives and Jerome F. Ryan Estate; 63: N. Currier/Library of Congress; 65: Courtesy of the General Mills Archives and Jerome F. Ryan Estate; 66: Frank Leslie's Illustrated Newspaper/Library of Congress; 67: Library of Congress; 69: Courtesy of the General Mills Archives and Jerome F. Ryan Estate; 71: Library of Congress; 72: Currier & Ives/Library of Congress; 74: Courtesy of the General Mills Archives and Jerome F. Ryan Estate; 75: Library of Congress; 77: Courtesy of the General Mills Archives and Jerome F. Ryan Estate; 78: Library of Congress; 79: Library of Congress; 81: Courtesy of the General Mills Archives and Jerome F. Ryan Estate; 82: Currier & Ives/Library of Congress; 83: Library of Congress; 84: Courtesy of the General Mills Archives and Jerome F. Ryan Estate; 85: Library of Congress; 87: Courtesy of the General Mills Archives and Jerome F. Ryan Estate; 88: Joseph Ferdinand Keppler/Library of Congress; 90: Courtesy of the General Mills Archives and Jerome F. Ryan Estate; 91: Thure de Thulstrup/Library of Congress; 93: Courtesy of the General Mills Archives and Jerome F. Ryan Estate; 94: George Prince/Library of Congress; 95: Hulton Archive/Getty Images; 96: Courtesy of the General Mills Archives and Jerome F. Ryan Estate; 98: Courtesy of the General Mills Archives and Jerome F. Ryan Estate; 99: Harris & Ewing/Library of Congress; 100: Library of Congress; 101: Library of Congress; 102: Courtesy of the General Mills Archives and Jerome F. Ryan Estate; 103: Library of Congress; 105: Courtesy of the General Mills Archives and Jerome F. Ryan Estate; 106: Library of Congress; 109: Courtesy of the General Mills Archives and Jerome F. Ryan Estate; 111: Courtesy of the General Mills Archives and Jerome F. Ryan Estate; 112: Everett Collection Inc/Alamy Images; 113: Harris & Ewing/Library of Congress; 114: Library of Congress; 115: Courtesy of the General Mills Archives and Jerome F. Ryan Estate; 116: Harris & Ewing/Library of Congress; 117: Harris & Ewing/Library of Congress; 119: Courtesy of the General Mills Archives and Jerome F. Ryan Estate; 120: FDR Presidential Library & Museum; 121: Harris & Ewing/Library of Congress; 122: Library of Congress; 124: Courtesy of the General Mills Archives and Jerome F. Ryan Estate; 125: United States Army Air Force/Library of Congress; 126: Library of Congress; 128: Courtesy of the General Mills Archives and Jerome F. Ryan Estate; 129: Bettmann/Getty Images; 130: John F. Kennedy Presidential Library and Museum; 132: Courtesy of the General Mills Archives and Jerome F. Ryan Estate; 133: AP Images; 134: NASA; 136: Courtesy of the General Mills Archives and Jerome F. Ryan Estate; 137: Bettmann/Getty Images; 139: Courtesy of the General Mills Archives and Jerome F. Ryan Estate; 141: Richard Nixon Library; 143: Courtesy of the General Mills Archives and Jerome F. Ryan Estate; 144: Marlon S. Trikosko/Library of Congress; 146: Courtesy of the General Mills Archives and Jerome F. Ryan Estate; 148: Bettmann/Getty Images; 150: Library of Congress; 151: Ronald Reagan Presidential Library; 152: AP Images; 154: David Valdez/Library of Congress; 155: George H. W. Bush Presidential Library and Museum; 156: George H. W. Bush Presidential Library and Museum; 158: Library of Congress; 159: William J. Clinton Presidential Library; 160: William J. Clinton Presidential Library; 164: National Archives and Records Administration; 165: Courtesy George W. Bush Presidential Library and Museum; 167: National Archives and Records Administration; 169: Courtesy George W. Bush Presidential Library and Museum; 172: Pete Souza/Library of Congress; 174: Steve Liss/The LIFE Images Collection/Getty Images; 177: White House Photo; 178: White House Photo; 182: Carrienelson1/Dreamstime; 184: Dennis Caruso/New York Daily News Archive/Getty Images; 187: Joe McNally/Getty Images; 188: Sara D. Davis/Getty Images; 192: White House Photo.

ISBN-13: 978-1-338-03807-1
ISBN-10: 1-338-03807-9

Copyright © 2016 by George Sullivan
Copyright © 2009, 2005, 2001, 1997, 1992, 1989, 1984 by George Sullivan.
Previously published under the title Mr. President.

10 9 8 7 6 5 4 3 2 1   16 17 18 19 20

Printed in the U.S.A.   40
First edition, December 2016
Book design by Maeve Norton

CONTENTS

Barack and Michelle Obama dancing at his inaguration ball.

Some Facts About
ELECTING THE PRESIDENT

Every four years, on January 20, a new or a reelected president of the United States is sworn into office. With their left hand on an open Bible and their right hand raised, they take the oath of office from the Chief Justice of the U.S. Supreme Court.

The inauguration ceremony is the result of a process that began sometimes years before, when the newly elected president announced his or her intention to be a candidate. Several people may declare themselves as candidates in one of the many political parties.

Whatever their qualifications, however, candidates must first win their party's nomination. To gain support, they will debate, speak before various groups, and meet the public and the press on various issues. Once nominated, a candidate must campaign for election, seeking to win the approval of the voters. From nomination to inauguration is, today, a long, hard fight.

WHO CAN BECOME PRESIDENT

The Constitution says that a candidate for the presidency must be a United States citizen from birth. (A naturalized citizen cannot be a candidate.) A candidate must also be at least 35 years old and have lived in the United States for at least 14 years. (These are the requirements. To qualify, most presidential candidates will have proved their leadership, usually through their record in public office.)

HOW A CANDIDATE IS NOMINATED

To be chosen as a candidate, a person must run against one or more other members of his or her political party. The two major political parties, the Democrats and Republicans, use primary elections, caucuses, and national conventions in selecting their nominees.

PRIMARIES AND CAUCUSES

Through the winter and spring of the election year, each of the major political parties holds a series of primaries. These are preliminary elections held by the states to choose delegates to the national conventions. Most of the delegates selected are pledged to vote for the presidential candidate chosen by the voters.

States offer either open or closed primaries. An open primary is an election in which any registered voter is eligible to vote.

A closed primary is one in which only voters who are registered with a particular party can vote. Only Democrats can vote in a Democratic primary; only Republicans can vote in a Republican primary.

The caucus is the oldest method of choosing candidates. Usually held at a community center, school, church, or library, a caucus is a meeting of voters in which delegates to the Democratic or Republican national conventions are chosen. In most cases, only people who are registered members of a political party can attend caucuses and vote.

Since 1972, the state of Iowa has held the nation's first caucus each election year. There were close to 2,000 Iowa caucuses for each party in 2016, each a kind of mini nominating convention.

SUPER TUESDAY

On a Tuesday in February or March of each presidential election year, a large number of states hold primary contests, which makes that Tuesday of "super" importance to the candidates since it is the

Ronald Reagan on the campaign trail.

day when the highest number of delegates are awarded. On Super Tuesday in 2016, Republican Donald Trump won seven of the eleven states holding primaries. The large number of delegates awarded to Trump on that day made it mathematically impossible for any other candidate to catch up with him and get to the 1,237 delegates necessary to become the Republican nominee.

THE CONVENTIONS

In the summer before the presidential election in November, each major party holds its national convention. While each convention is a week-long political circus, with stirring speechmaking, wild cheering, and parading delegates, the process of choosing a candidate is the first order of business.

Senator John F. Kennedy, center, of Massachusetts stops in a diner in Nashua, New Hampshire, during the New Hampshire primary campaign.

Since conventions are nationally televised, each is an opportunity for a party to present its most notable members and possible candidates for the future. During the Democratic convention in 2004, little-known Barack Obama, then a candidate for senator from the state of Illinois, delivered the party's keynote address, summing up what the Democrats stood for. Obama dazzled both the convention delegates and TV viewers. In November, Obama was elected to the U.S. Senate and four years later was a presidential candidate himself.

In 2016, a total of 2,472 delegates were expected to attend the Republican convention. To win the nomination, a candidate had to receive at least 1,237 votes.

On the Democratic side, there were 4,765 delegates. To win, 2,383 were needed.

Among the Democratic delegates, 719 were designated super-delegates. Those named superdelegates were members of Congress, governors, former presidents, and party officials. President Obama was a superdelegate in 2016.

Superdelegates, which are typically only important on the Democratic side, are not pledged to follow the will of the voters. They are unbound, meaning they can vote for whoever they choose.

SMALL-PARTY CANDIDATES

Usually one or more of the smaller national parties offers candidates for president, too. In 1992, for example, H. Ross Perot of Texas, a billionaire businessman, ran as an independent candidate. He received more than 19 million votes, which amounted to about 19 percent of the total votes cast. But he failed to capture any electoral votes.

In the 2012 election, Gary Johnson, the presidential candidate of the Libertarian Party, attracted slightly less than 1 percent of the total votes cast.

THE CAMPAIGN

Once the national parties have chosen their candidates, the presidential race heats up. A campaign manager coordinates operations for each nominee. Political consultants conduct voter research and advise on strategy. Volunteers are organized and a huge network of supporters is put together.

The main points a candidate wants to impress upon the voters are crafted into a consistent message. Day in and day out, throughout his successful run for the presidency in 2008, Barack Obama delivered a constant message of "change" that had great voter appeal.

Each candidate crisscrosses the country, getting out the message at mass meetings, rallies, and other public forums. In reciting the message, the media gets special attention. The term "media" used to mean TV, radio, and print newspapers. Not anymore. Its role has deepened and broadened. Digital communication has expanded to social media and news media. Social media—like Facebook, Twitter, Pinterest, and Instagram—is a free or low-cost and highly effective method of winning support, especially among younger voters.

The presidential debates play a vital role in the campaign. There are three of them, and they are televised. Doing well can give an important boost to one's candidacy. Doing poorly can be fatal to victory.

On Election Day, everyone works to get people to vote. More than 130 million Americans vote for presidential candidates.

For the candidates, the campaign is a grueling experience. But getting elected does not provide much of a break. On January 20, about ten weeks after the election, the winner is sworn in as the next president.

SOCIAL MEDIA

During the 2016 presidential campaign, Hillary Clinton's team used Snapchat to share a 1965 photo of Hillary in high school and wished

While campaigning for his second term as president in February 1996,
Bill Clinton holds a baby and greets voters along State Street in Concord, New Hampshire.

students a "Happy first day of school." The post wasn't meant to enlist student support for her election; Snapchat isn't permitted to post campaign materials. The intention was to create an image around Mrs. Clinton, to make her easier to relate to.

This is just one example of the wide range of social media outlets used by the Clinton team during her campaign in 2016. In the summer leading up to the November election, she had more than five million "Likes" on Facebook and eight million-plus Twitter followers. She had accounts on Instagram and Pinterest, and her team even created a Spotify playlist that voters could listen to.

Candidates use social media for many different reasons. During the 2016 campaign, Donald Trump, a Republican, relied on Periscope to announce his candidacy. Rand Paul, also a Republican, produced ads on Snapchat that reported his views on the U.S. tax code. Republican John Kasich used a ten-second Snapchat ad to promote his campaign in Iowa. And Republican Jeb Bush ran video clips on Instagram to hail the launch of his Super Political Action Committee fund-raiser.

The political media that was such a vital part of the 2016 election process, and the term "social media" itself, didn't exist until recent times. George Bush won the presidency in 2000 the old-fashioned way, using TV, radio, and newspapers to get his message across. The term "social media" wasn't used in the mainstream until 2004, the same year Facebook was born. Twitter dates to 2006. Apple introduced the iPhone, one of the earliest smartphones, in 2007. Smartphones enable their users to gain instant access to the Internet and social media via apps. By the time of the 2016 election, there were over one hundred million iPhones in use in the United States alone.

Barack Obama, in defeating Hillary Clinton in the race to be the Democratic nominee in 2008, was the first candidate to use social media as a meaningful campaign strategy. He had over twenty million Facebook followers that year.

ELECTION DAY

Election Day is the first Tuesday after the first Monday in November. It is a legal holiday in most states. Beginning in the early morning hours, voters go to the "polls," rooms in designated buildings in neighborhood districts called voting "precincts." (There are 166,000 voting precincts in the United States.)

In the earliest method of voting, each voter received a paper ballot from an election clerk. The voter took the ballot into a private booth, marked it with his or her choices, folded it, and then slipped it into a ballot box.

In most areas of the country, paper ballots have been replaced by voting machines. In these, voters press buttons or move levers to indicate their choices. Electronic voting systems are also growing in popularity. In one type of electronic system, paper cards are marked by hand and then counted electronically. In others, the voter presses buttons or uses a touch screen to register his or her vote. U.S. citizens who are eighteen or older are eligible to vote.

After the polling places close, the votes are counted. Paper ballots are counted by hand. Electronic voting machines tabulate votes automatically. Once the vote counting is completed, the nation has what's called the "popular vote." When Barack Obama was re-elected in 2012, he received 65,915,795 popular votes and earned 332 electoral votes.

THE ELECTORAL VOTE

Strictly speaking, people don't elect the president. The states do. This happens through the use of the Electoral College and the electoral voting system.

When Americans vote for president, they are actually voting for presidential electors. As a group, the electors are known as the Electoral College.

For each state, the number of votes is the same as the total of its Senators plus its members of the House of Representatives. For example, Florida, with two Senators and twenty-seven House Representative members, has twenty-nine total electoral votes.

In all, there are a total of 538 electors. Each has one vote. In most states, the candidate who wins the popular vote in a state gets all of that state's electoral votes. At least 270 votes—a majority—are required to win the presidency.

Since the number of members in each state's House of Representatives delegation is based on the state's population, the states with the most people have the most electoral votes. California, the most populated state, has 55 electoral votes. Texas, second to California, has 38.

The states with the fewest electoral votes are Delaware, Montana, North Dakota, South Dakota, Vermont, and Wyoming. Each has three electoral votes, as does the District of Columbia.

CLIFFHANGERS

The electoral system usually works well—except in very close elections. Then the candidate with the most popular votes may fail to win enough electoral votes to be declared the winner. It's the "losing" candidate who wins. Chaos is the result. This has happened several times:

• 1824—For the four leading candidates, the electoral vote totals looked like this:

Candidate	Electoral Vote
Andrew Jackson	99 votes
John Quincy Adams	84 votes
William Crawford	41 votes
Henry Clay	37 votes

Since no candidate received a majority of the electoral votes, it fell to the House of Representatives to choose a president. The House decided on John Quincy Adams (which thoroughly shocked Andrew Jackson).

• 1876—In the popular vote, Democrat Samuel Tilden of New York was the clear winner over Ohio's Rutherford B. Hayes, a Republican.

Candidate	Popular Vote	Electoral Vote
Samuel Tilden	4,300,590	184
Rutherford B. Hayes	4,036,298	165

Neither candidate, however, had the required number of electoral votes—185. The electoral votes in South Carolina, Florida, and Louisiana were disputed. Congress set up a fifteen-member commission to end the standoff. After much political maneuvering, the commission voted in favor of Hayes.

• 1888—Grover Cleveland, a Democrat, piled up big majorities in the states that supported him. Republican Benjamin Harrison captured his states by the slimmest of margins. Nevertheless, he managed to put together an electoral majority and became the nation's 23rd president.

Candidate	Popular Vote	Electoral Vote
Grover Cleveland	5,537,857	168
Benjamin Harrison	5,447,129	233

The election of 1888 is looked upon as the classic example of the "wrong" winner winning.

• 2000—In one of the most bitterly contested elections, Republican George W. Bush captured a majority of the electoral votes, while Democratic candidate Al Gore received the greatest number of popular votes.

Candidate	Popular Vote	Electoral Vote
Al Gore	51,003,894	266
George W. Bush	50,459,211	271

With over 100 million votes cast, it was an unusually close election. On the morning after the election, the outcome was still in doubt. Each candidate needed Florida's 25 electoral votes to win. But in several Florida counties, the vote was disputed. The final result hung in the balance for weeks as Florida's votes were counted and recounted. The controversy over delegates was finally resolved in Bush's favor by a decision of the U.S. Supreme Court.

While elections that are nail-biters cause great anxiety, the electoral system works reliably any time one candidate gets a clear majority of both the popular and electoral votes. The biggest landslide in presidential election history took place in 1964, when Democrat Lyndon Johnson defeated Republican Barry Goldwater. Johnson got 486 of 538—90.3 percent—of the electoral votes. In the history of big presidential landslides, Johnson's victory is at the top of the list. Afterward, there was no confusion, no dispute, and no criticism of the electoral system.

RED VS. BLUE

Anyone watching the election coverage on TV realizes that results are usually reported in terms of red states and blue states. A map depicts each state in one of those two colors. A red state favors the Republican candidate, a blue state, the Democratic one. These labels have been widely used since the presidential election of 2000. Red and blue

The inauguration of Abraham Lincoln.

states are termed "safe" states; there's no doubt as to which candidate the voters in those states prefer, but there are purple states, too. These are states in which neither candidate has a clear-cut majority of votes (purple being a combination of red and blue). Such states are also called swing states, meaning that they can turn—"swing"—toward either the Democratic or Republican party. Colorado, Florida, Ohio, Virginia, and Nevada are often cited as swing states.

THE PRESIDENT IN OFFICE

INAUGURATION DAY

At noon on January 20th following Election Day, the new president-elect stands on the Capitol steps in Washington, DC, and takes the oath of office. At the moment he or she finishes the oath, that person becomes the president of the United States.

OATH OF OFFICE

"I do solemnly swear (or affirm) that I will faithfully execute the Office of President of the United States, and will, to the best of my ability, preserve, protect, and defend the Constitution of the United States."

—from Article II, Section 1, U.S. Constitution

WHAT THE PRESIDENT DOES

The Constitution grants the president enormous powers. Those powers have grown through the years. Today, the president of the United States is the most powerful elected official in the world.

As the nation's chief executive, it is the president's job to make sure all federal laws are enforced. He or she makes proposals for new laws and urges Congress to act upon them.

The White House.

The president is commander in chief of the army, navy, air force, and marines, and speaks for our country in dealing with foreign nations.

The president nominates Supreme Court judges, ambassadors, and other high officials. However, these nominations must be approved by the majority rule of the Senate.

VETO POWER OF THE PRESIDENT

The power to make laws is shared by the president and Congress. When Congress passes a law, the president can either sign it or veto it. The president's veto kills the law unless Congress repasses it by a two-thirds vote. Vetoes are seldom overridden.

As leader of his or her political party, the president has taken on powers not spelled out in the Constitution. For example, most presidents have enough control within their party to get themselves renominated easily.

If a president does not choose to run, he or she can usually pick a candidate to run in their place.

THE CABINET

Also available to assist the president are the heads of 15 executive departments of the government. When these 15 officials plus the vice president meet as a group, they are known as the cabinet. The cabinet offices are:

Secretary of State
Secretary of the Treasury
Secretary of Defense
Secretary of Homeland Security
Attorney General
Secretary of Transportation
Secretary of the Interior
Secretary of Energy
Secretary of Agriculture
Secretary of Commerce

Secretary of Labor
Secretary of Health and
    Human Services
Secretary of Health and
    Human Services
Secretary of Housing and
    Urban Development
Secretary of Education
Secretary of Veterans Affairs

President Grover Cleveland meeting with cabinet members.

GEORGE WASHINGTON

1st President

Born: February 22, 1732

Birthplace: Pope's Creek, Westmoreland County, Virginia

Previous experience: Surveyor, farmer, delegate to the Continental Congress, first commander in chief

Political party: None

Term of office: April 30, 1789– March 3, 1797

Died: December 14, 1799

Some people wanted George Washington to be King George of the new United States. But Washington had just fought a long war to free America from a king's tight rule. He wanted no kings in America, and he wanted to set a good precedent as the nation's first leader. Very soon, the proper title for the nation's chief executive became "Mr. President."

Born on the family farm in Virginia, young Washington was raised on land that his great-grandfather, a native of England, had settled. At 15, he was a big-boned young man who was good in arithmetic; he became a surveyor. Later, he commanded the colony's soldiers guarding Virginia's frontiers against French and Indian raiders. When the raids developed into the French and Indian War, Washington became an aide to British general Edward Braddock. At 27, he had married Martha Custis, a young widow with two children, and he

A painting of President Washington and his family by Edward Savage.

looked forward to life as a gentleman farmer. Like many colonists, however, Washington suffered from British regulations and taxes, and he spoke out firmly against them.

And when the growing American resistance was met by British troops, America's Second Continental Congress called for military force.

THE CONGRESS ELECTED WASHINGTON TO BE COMMANDER IN CHIEF OF THE AMERICAN FORCES.

For seven long years, Washington held together his ragtag army— now slipping away from the enemy to launch a surprise attack; now retreating, in the winter cold, to Valley Forge. Many soldiers gave up and went home. But Washington hung on, losing more battles than he won. Eventually, with French aid, he forced the British to surrender.

Washington turned with relief to his beloved home and long-

A painting by Emanuel Leutze of Christmas Day in 1776, when Washington led his army across the Delaware River to New Jersey to launch a surprise attack against 1,400 Hessian soldiers at Trenton early on December 26th.

neglected farm at Mount Vernon, Virginia. But he realized that if the new nation was to be strong, it needed a binding contract with all the states. Washington called for a Constitutional Convention to meet in Philadelphia in 1787 to write the Constitution.

After the Constitution was approved by the states, the graying hero, 57 years old, was unanimously elected the country's first president. Washington chose two famous men to help him. Thomas Jefferson became America's first secretary of state and Alexander Hamilton the first secretary of the treasury.

At last, after serving two terms, a worn and weary Washington retired to Mount Vernon for good. As its first commander in chief, president, and founder, Washington had been a true father of our country, helping it grow from 13 separate colonies into a free nation.

GEORGE WASHINGTON
Important Events

1789 – Department of Foreign Affairs (State Department), Department of War, Treasury Department, Post Office Department, and Office of the Attorney General established

1790 – First session of U.S. Supreme Court

1790 – First U.S. census authorized

1791 – District of Columbia established

1791 – Vermont admitted as the 14th state

1791 – First ten amendments to the Constitution — the Bill of Rights — ratified

1792 – Kentucky admitted as the 15th state

1792 – Cornerstone of the executive mansion laid

1793 – Cornerstone of the Capitol laid

1794 – Eli Whitney patented the cotton gin

1796 – Tennessee admitted as the 16th state

JOHN ADAMS

2nd President

Born: October 30, 1735

Birthplace: Massachusetts

Previous experience: Lawyer, delegate to Continental Congress, diplomat, vice president

Political party: Federalist

Term of office: March 4, 1797– March 3, 1801

Died: July 4, 1826

A short, plump New Englander, John Adams was responsible for many noteworthy achievements during America's struggle for freedom. But because he lived in an age of great leaders, he was frequently overshadowed in what he did.

Harvard-educated lawyer John Adams was a patriot in Massachusetts in the years before the Revolution, although his fiery cousin, Samuel Adams, made a bigger stir. Typical of John Adams's sense of justice, he defended in court the British soldiers who fired into a patriotic Boston mob, because he felt everyone deserved a fair trial.

In the Continental Congress, he was assigned to the committee to write the Declaration of Independence. He had led the movement for such a declaration, but he was upstaged by Thomas Jefferson, who actually penned the great document.

As a diplomat in France during the Revolutionary War, Adams was outshone by the urbane and genial Benjamin Franklin. However,

Adams helped negotiate the treaty of peace and was later a minister to the Court of St. James in England.

Finally, Adams was the nation's first vice president—to the great President Washington. "The most insignificant office that ever the invention of man contrived," Adams wrote of his job to his beloved wife, Abigail.

ADAMS BECAME PRESIDENT IN 1797—A VERY TROUBLED TIME FOR THE YOUNG NATION.

France attacked some of our ships. Many people, led by Alexander Hamilton, wanted Adams to declare war against France. But he resolutely held that the young nation should not fight. He sent a peace mission to France, a decision that may have cost him reelection.

Adams was the first president to live in the new capital city of Washington, DC, and the first to occupy the executive mansion. Only six rooms were ready when he and his wife moved in. Mrs. Adams hung her washing in the empty East Room.

John Adams's wife, Abigail Adams.

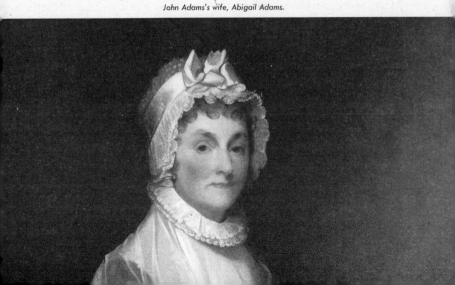

When Adams's single term of office ended, he retired to his farm in Quincy, Massachusetts. He lived long enough to see a son, John Quincy, become president.

Adams wrote many letters to Jefferson. The friendly rivalry of these two patriots ended in 1826, when both men died on the Fourth of July.

JOHN ADAMS
Important Events

1797 – First naval vessel, *United States*, launched in Philadelphia

1798 – Mississippi Territory created

1798 – Department of the Navy created

1798 – Marine Corps created

1800 – Library of Congress established

1800 – Capital moved to Washington, DC

THOMAS JEFFERSON

3rd President

Born: April 13, 1743

Birthplace: Shadwell, Virginia

Previous experience: Delegate to Continental Congress, governor, diplomat, secretary of state, vice president

Political party: Democratic-Republican

Term of office: March 4, 1801– March 3, 1809

Died: July 4, 1826

For forty years, the remarkable Thomas Jefferson devoted himself to public service—but he also found time to be a successful lawyer, farmer, architect, musician, and inventor.

Jefferson had many skills. He spoke six languages, including Latin and Greek. He loved gadgets and once built a clock that ran on cannon balls as weights. The tall, red-headed Jefferson could break a horse, dance a minuet, and play the violin.

He was admired as a writer and a thinker. In 1776 he was picked to head the Declaration of Independence committee, and Jefferson wrote the draft himself.

PROCLAIMING "ALL MEN ARE CREATED EQUAL," THE DECLARATION IS OFTEN CALLED THE MOST IMPORTANT DOCUMENT IN AMERICAN HISTORY.

A painting by John Trumbull of Thomas Jefferson signing the Declaration of Independence.

Three years later, Governor Jefferson established religious liberty in Virginia and introduced free education and public libraries in that state.

When Jefferson became president, he sent James Monroe and Robert Livingston to France to arrange the purchase of New Orleans and West Florida. Napoleon, who needed war funds, offered and sold the men an enormous tract of land that ran from the Mississippi River to the Rocky Mountains. This real estate bargain, at three cents per acre, was called the Louisiana Purchase; it doubled the size of the country.

Jefferson also ordered the Lewis and Clark expedition to explore what is now the northwestern part of the United States.

After leaving the presidency, Jefferson retired to Monticello, the home he had designed, and devoted his remaining years to the founding of the University of Virginia. One of the best tributes ever paid to Jefferson came from one of his presidential successors—John F. Kennedy. Kennedy was playing host to a group of men and women who had been honored for their outstanding achievements in art and science. Kennedy described his guests as the most extraordinary collection of talent that had ever been gathered together at the White House, with the possible exception of Thomas Jefferson—when he dined alone.

Monticello, the beautiful home in Virginia that Jefferson designed and built, stands today as a monument to his varied interests and talents.

THOMAS JEFFERSON
Important Events

1802 – U.S. Military Academy authorized

1803 – Ohio admitted as the 17th state

1803 – Louisiana Purchase treaty signed

1803 – Lewis and Clark left St. Louis on their expedition
to the Pacific

1809 – Illinois Territory established

FUN FACT:
FOUR STATE CAPITALS HAVE BEEN NAMED
FOR PRESIDENTS. THEY ARE: JACKSON,
MISSISSIPPI; JEFFERSON CITY, MISSOURI;
LINCOLN, NEBRASKA; AND MADISON, WISCONSIN.

JAMES MADISON

4th President

Born: March 16, 1751

Birthplace: Port Conway, Virginia

Previous experience: Lawyer, delegate to Continental Congress, congressman, secretary of state

Political party: Democratic-Republican

Term of office: March 4, 1809– March 3, 1817

Died: June 28, 1836

One of our smallest presidents, the brilliant Virginian James Madison stood only 5 feet, 4 inches and never weighed more than 100 pounds. At his inauguration, he looked like a little old man beside his blooming wife, Dolley. Yet Madison was one of the "Big Four" from Virginia. Like Monroe, Jefferson, and Washington, he helped lead Congress and the nation during America's formative years.

Right after the Revolutionary War, the states began quarreling among themselves. Madison believed we needed a strong national government to survive. More than anyone else, he created the Constitution and urged its adoption by the states.

Madison also fought to add the first ten amendments to the Constitution. Known as the Bill of Rights, these amendments protect such liberties as freedom of speech, freedom of the press, freedom of religion, and the right to a trial by jury.

An engraving of *Dolley Madison* by *Evert A. Duyckinick.*

This work was all behind Madison when in 1794, at the age of 43, he met and married a young, pretty widow, Dolley Payne Todd. When Madison took over as president in 1809, Dolley became a popular hostess, known for her gala parties. At these parties, many people had their first taste of a new dessert called "ice cream."

During Madison's first term as president, the young nation's ships were seized at sea by warring France and England. America's quarrel with England over freedom of the seas led to the War of 1812. In a surprise raid on Washington, British marines set fire to public buildings and burned the executive mansion. Madison and his wife fled to the Virginia woods. Dolley paused long enough to carry away a valuable portrait of George Washington.

When the Madisons returned to Washington after the war, they had to live in temporary quarters until the executive mansion was rebuilt.

WHITE PAINT WAS USED TO COVER THE FIRE-BLACKENED EXTERIOR, AND FROM THEN ON IT WAS KNOWN AS THE WHITE HOUSE.

Retiring from the White House in 1817, Madison returned to his home in Montpelier, Virginia. He died in 1836 at the age of 85; he had outlived all the other founders of the nation.

JAMES MADISON
Important Events

1811 – General William Henry Harrison defeated Indian attackers at battle of Tippecanoe

1812 – Louisiana admitted as the 18th state

1812 – Missouri Territory organized

1812 – War declared against Great Britain

1814 – "The Star-Spangled Banner" composed by Francis Scott Key

1814 – Peace treaty signed with Great Britain

1816 – Indiana admitted as the 19th state

5th President

Born: April 28, 1758

Birthplace: Westmoreland County, Virginia

Previous experience: Soldier, lawyer, delegate to Continental Congress, senator, governor, diplomat, secretary of state, secretary of war

Political party: Democratic-Republican

Term of office: March 4, 1817– March 3, 1825

Died: July 4, 1831

J ames Monroe always seemed to be where the action was. When the Revolutionary War broke out, Monroe was 18. A Virginia planter's son, he was attending William and Mary College, but quit school to join General Washington's army in New York. Six months later, as Lieutenant Monroe, he crossed the Delaware with Washington and then fought in the hard battles of Brandywine, Germantown, and Monmouth.

AT TRENTON, A BULLET STRUCK HIM AND REMAINED IN HIS SHOULDER FOR THE REST OF HIS LIFE.

After the revolution, Monroe studied law with Thomas Jefferson and entered politics. He was elected to the U.S. Senate, then became minister to France and helped negotiate the Louisiana Purchase, by which France sold America enough land to double the size of our

36

country. Back home, Monroe was twice elected governor of Virginia, and later served as secretary of state.

The popular Monroe was elected president in 1816, and reelected in 1820 almost unanimously by an electoral vote of 231 to 1. (The single vote against him was cast by a New Hampshire delegate who wanted George Washington to have the honor of being the only unanimous choice in history.)

As president, Monroe's greatest successes took place in the field he knew best—foreign policy. When Spain cast a longing eye on Central and South American countries that had become newly independent, Monroe told the Spanish and other European nations, "Hands off." He declared that the United States would permit no "foreign interference" in the New World. We remember James Monroe best for this Monroe Doctrine.

The Battle of Trenton by Charles McBarron.

JAMES MONROE
Important Events

1817 – Mississippi admitted as the 20th state

1818 – Illinois admitted as the 21st state

1819 – Florida purchased from Spain

1819 – First American steamship crossed the Atlantic

1819 – Alabama admitted as the 22nd state

1820 – Maine admitted as the 23rd state

1821 – Missouri admitted as the 24th state

1823 – Monroe Doctrine proclaimed

JOHN QUINCY ADAMS

6th President

Born: July 11, 1767

Birthplace: Braintree, Massachusetts

Previous experience: Lawyer, diplomat, senator, secretary of state, congressman

Political party: Democratic-Republican

Term of office: March 4, 1825–March 3, 1829

Died: February 23, 1848

John Quincy Adams was the first president who was also the son of a president. His father was John Adams.

Both Adamses were born in Braintree, Massachusetts, in houses that stood next to each other. They both went to Harvard College, became lawyers, and lived in the same houses in their later years. Both were short and as stubborn as mules.

Both served as diplomats, helping to write peace treaties to end war with England—John Adams after the Revolutionary War and John Quincy Adams after the War of 1812—and each served only one term as president.

John Quincy Adams was one of the great secretaries of state. Serving under Monroe, he made agreements on lands with Spain and England, and helped Monroe formulate the Monroe Doctrine.

The John Adams house in Braintree, Massachusetts where John Quincy Adams grew up.

As president, John Quincy Adams lived a plain life. He rose each morning at five o'clock, built his own fire, read his Bible, and bathed in the Potomac—before anyone else in the capital was awake.

ONE TIME, WHILE HE WAS TAKING HIS MORNING DIP, A THIEF RAN OFF WITH HIS CLOTHES.

The president had to ask a passing boy to dash up to the White House and ask Mrs. Adams for something to wear.

Adams had a troubled term in office. He had to work with a hostile Congress that blocked most of his plans. His program to encourage interest and education in the arts and sciences had some success,

 40

however. He was able to get the important Smithsonian Institution established.

Adams was defeated for reelection by Andrew Jackson in 1828. But he was not retired for long. When his neighbors asked him if he would be willing to represent their district in Congress, Adams said yes.

The debate on slavery was beginning to heat up. With Adams in Congress, it got much hotter. He hated slavery. For eight years, he argued in Congress against owning slaves. Other congressmen tried to silence him.

Adams kept talking—until one day in 1848. At the age of 80, while waiting for still another chance to speak in the House of Representatives against slavery, Adams collapsed from a stroke. Two days later he died.

JOHN QUINCY ADAMS
Important Events

1825 – Erie Canal opened for traffic

1828 – Construction began on Baltimore & Ohio railroad

ANDREW JACKSON

7th President

Born: March 15, 1767

Birthplace: Waxhaw District, South Carolina

Previous experience: Lawyer, congressman, military leader, governor, senator

Political party: Democrat

Term of office: March 4, 1829– March 3, 1837

Died: June 8, 1845

After General Andrew Jackson won the presidency in 1828, the farmers, working men, and frontiersmen who supported him swarmed to Washington. They perched on rooftops and packed sidewalks to catch a glimpse of him on Inauguration Day. After the ceremony, these men in their coonskin caps and muddy boots pushed their way into the White House. They toppled punch bowls and stood on satin-covered chairs to cheer the new president. "The reign of king mob," one observer called it.

No doubt about it, Andrew Jackson gave a new direction to the presidency. From Washington to John Quincy Adams, the presidents had been gentlemen of money and privilege. Jackson changed that. He represented the plain, common people.

JACKSON WAS THE FIRST PRESIDENT TO BE BORN IN A LOG CABIN AND THE FIRST FROM THE NEW WEST.

As an unschooled orphan of 13, he fought in the Revolutionary War. When he was taken prisoner, he refused to clean a British officer's boots, and for that he received a saber blow that left a scar on his forehead for life.

At the age of 20, Jackson was a backwoods lawyer. Ten years later, he was a strong political figure in the newly formed state of Tennessee, and held the office of U.S. senator.

In the War of 1812, the hotheaded, hawk-nosed Jackson became a national hero, first as an Indian fighter, and then in the Battle of New Orleans.

After his great victory over the British at New Orleans, people began mentioning Jackson as a future president. In 1824 he was defeated by John Quincy Adams, but four years later Jackson beat Adams by a clear

A painting of Andrew Jackson at the Battle of New Orleans by Percy Moran.

margin. At his moment of glory, however, Jackson was plunged into sorrow. His beloved wife, Rachel, died just as Jackson was preparing to leave for Washington.

In his first year as president, Jackson removed some two thousand federal officeholders and gave their jobs to his followers. He battled the Bank of the United States, calling it a bank of the rich.

Jackson was a Southerner, but when the Southern state of South Carolina threatened to leave the Union in a squabble over tariffs, Jackson would not permit it. "Our Union—it must be preserved," he declared.

Reelected in 1832, Jackson continued his fight as the people's champion. Four years later he retired to the home he had built near Nashville, Tennessee—the Hermitage. There he lies in a simple grave.

ANDREW JACKSON
Important Events

1836 – Arkansas admitted as the 25th state

1836 – Wisconsin Territory organized

1836 – Republic of Texas recognized

1837 – Michigan admitted as the 26th state

MARTIN VAN BUREN

8th President

Born: December 5, 1782

Birthplace: Kinderhook, New York

Previous experience: Lawyer, senator, governor, secretary of state, vice president

Political party: Democrat

Term of office: March 4, 1837– March 3, 1841

Died: July 24, 1862

O ur first seven presidents were born in what had been colonial America. Martin Van Buren was the first president born in the new United States. Even so, "Little Van" grew up speaking Dutch better than English. His ancestors came from the Netherlands, and he was raised in the old Dutch village of Kinderhook, New York.

His father owned a tavern that was a convenient stopping place for politicians traveling from New York City to Albany, and young Van Buren met the political leaders of the day there. At 14, he took a job as a law clerk, and at 20, he set up his own successful law practice.

Van Buren was even more successful as a politician. He was always ready with a smile, a handshake, and a joke. He became so skilled in achieving his political goals that he was nicknamed the "Little Magician."

In 1828 Van Buren worked his magic for Andrew Jackson, helping him to become president. In turn, Jackson made Van Buren his secretary of state and later, his vice president. Jackson also supported him when Van Buren ran for the presidency in 1836.

Van Buren had been in office only two months when the nation was struck by the financial panic of 1837. Banks closed one after another, mill towns shut down, and workers lost their jobs.

THE UNEMPLOYED RIOTED IN NEW YORK. VAN BUREN, BELIEVING THE GOVERNMENT SHOULD NOT INTERFERE IN PRIVATE BUSINESS, DID LITTLE TO HELP.

By the time Van Buren sought reelection in 1840, he was terribly unpopular. To make matters worse, his rivals portrayed him as a man who drank wine from a silver goblet and ate his meals from gold plates. His opponent, William Henry Harrison, won easily.

Van Buren, the politician, never regained the support of the Democratic party. He was nominated by the Free Soil Party—a party opposed to slavery—in 1848. He did not win, however, and did not try again.

MARTIN VAN BUREN
Important Events

1837 - Patent for manufacture of rubber obtained by Charles Goodyear

1838 - Boundary treaty with Texas signed

1838 - Iowa territorial government authorized

FUN FACT:
MARTIN VAN BUREN, BORN ON DECEMBER 5, 1782, WAS THE FIRST PRESIDENT TO BE BORN A CITIZEN OF THE UNITED STATES. PREVIOUS PRESIDENTS HAD BEEN BORN BEFORE THE AMERICAN REVOLUTION, AND THUS WERE BORN BRITISH SUBJECTS.

WILLIAM HENRY HARRISON

9th President

Born: February 9, 1773

Birthplace: Berkeley, Virginia

Previous experience: Military leader, territorial governor, congressman, senator

Political party: Whig*

Term of office: March 4, 1841– April 4, 1841

Died: April 4, 1841

* * Party established about 1834 to oppose the Democrats.

Like Andrew Jackson, William Henry Harrison won fame because of his success as an Indian fighter and as a general during the War of 1812.

Born in Virginia, Harrison was the youngest child in a family of seven children. At 14, he entered college to study medicine, but had to give up his medical studies when his father died. He joined the army and headed to the northwest Indian frontier.

In 1801 Harrison became governor of the Indiana Territory (now Indiana and Illinois), and he held that post for twelve years. His main task was to obtain title to Indian lands for settlers moving west into the wilderness, and to defend the settlements against Indian raids.

The frontier Indians were up in arms because many millions of acres of hunting ground had been closed to them. Harrison met with their leaders and tried to cool their anger but without success.

Under the great Shawnee chief Tecumseh, the Indians formed a close confederation, and the raids continued against the settlers.

In 1811, with a force of about 800 volunteers, Harrison was headed toward an Indian town when the Indians attacked his camp on Tippecanoe Creek. Harrison repulsed them and later crushed Tecumseh's confederation. After the victory at Tippecanoe, "Old Tippecanoe" Harrison was hailed as a national hero.

Harrison served as a congressman and senator, and in 1840 the Whigs settled on him as a presidential candidate.

THEIR CAMPAIGN SLOGAN WAS "TIPPECANOE AND TYLER, TOO."

(John Tyler was the vice-presidential candidate.) Harrison and Tyler won in a landslide.

A print of the Battle of Tippecanoe by Alonzo Chappel.

The day of Harrison's inauguration was cold and rainy. Harrison, at 68, wanted to show he was in good health. He rode on horseback in the parade for two hours and took the oath of office bareheaded.

As a result, Harrison caught a cold that developed into pneumonia. He died on April 4, 1841, only 32 days after his inauguration. Harrison was the first president to die in office.

WILLIAM HENRY HARRISON
Important Events

Nothing of note happened in the United States during the 32 days Harrison was in office.

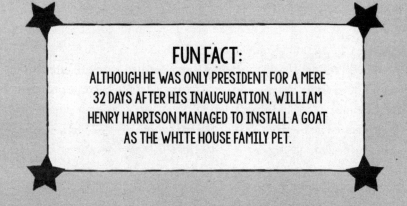

FUN FACT:
ALTHOUGH HE WAS ONLY PRESIDENT FOR A MERE 32 DAYS AFTER HIS INAUGURATION, WILLIAM HENRY HARRISON MANAGED TO INSTALL A GOAT AS THE WHITE HOUSE FAMILY PET.

10th President

Born: March 29, 1790

Birthplace: Charles City County, Virginia

Previous experience: Lawyer, congressman, governor, senator, vice president

Political party: Whig

Term of office: April 6, 1841– March 3, 1845

Died: January 18, 1862

John Tyler was the son of a plantation owner. A mild-mannered boy, he wrote and read poetry and enjoyed playing the violin. But he grew into a strong-minded, strong-willed adult. As president, he often opposed the leaders of Congress and his party.

Tyler was only 17 when he graduated from the College of William and Mary, and by 19, he was a practicing lawyer. Then he entered politics. After serving as a congressman, governor, and senator, Tyler became vice president in the election of 1840.

When President William Henry Harrison died a month after being inaugurated, Tyler became the first vice president to become president. At the time, some said that Tyler was only an "acting president." But Tyler insisted he be given the full title and granted full powers of office. Ever since then, on the death of the president, the vice president has been sworn in with full executive powers.

As president, Tyler's firmness soon brought him into conflict with Henry Clay and other leaders of his party. The Whigs wanted to set up a new national bank. They wanted high taxes on imported goods. When Tyler opposed these ideas, his cabinet resigned and the Whigs ousted Tyler.

HE WAS A PRESIDENT WITHOUT A PARTY.

Strong-minded President Tyler brought the war with the Seminole Indians in Florida to an end. He also entered into a treaty with China, which opened the way for trade with the countries of the Far East.

Tyler was the first president whose wife died while he was in office. When he remarried, he became the first president to marry while in office. He had fifteen children; no president has had more.

In 1845 Tyler retired to his estate in Virginia. When he died, he was still considered a rebel by the Whig leaders, who refused to make an official announcement of his death.

An engraving by William O. Stoddard of Tyler receiving the news of Harrison's death.

A painting of Tyler's first wife, Julia, by Francesco Anelli on the left, and an engraving of his second wife, Letitia, on the right by J. C. Buitre.

JOHN TYLER
Important Events

1842 – Treaty signed with Great Britain, settling U.S.-Canadian border in Maine and Minnesota Territory

1844 – First message sent over first telegraph line

1845 – Florida admitted as the 27th state

JAMES KNOX POLK

11th President

Born: November 2, 1795

Birthplace: Mecklenburg County, North Carolina

Previous experience: Lawyer, congressman, governor

Political party: Democrat

Term of office: March 4, 1845–March 3, 1849

Died: June 15, 1849

O ne of the very best, most honest, and most successful presidents the country ever had," was the way one historian described James Polk.

He was born in North Carolina and raised on the Tennessee frontier. In college, he never missed a class, and in his fourteen years as congressman, he was absent only once. He became Speaker of the House and was considered by most to be fair yet firm.

In 1844 Polk ran for president against the famous Senator Henry Clay.

POLK WAS SO LITTLE KNOWN THAT HE WAS CALLED A "DARK HORSE."

(At the racetrack, a dark horse is an unknown that unexpectedly wins.) In the election, Polk squeezed out a victory over Clay.

When Polk took office, there were only 27 states in the Union.

Much of the country was still Indian territory or claimed by foreign countries. "All of Texas and all of Oregon" had been Polk's campaign slogan. He settled the Oregon border by a treaty with Great Britain. But the dispute with Mexico over the Texas border was not settled so easily.

Polk sent troops into the disputed area. When they were fired upon, Polk was able to announce, "War exists by act of Mexico." American troops advanced into Mexican territory.

The Mexican War ended in 1848. Under the terms of the peace treaty, Mexico gave up all claims to Texas and territory that is now California and Nevada, and much of what is Arizona, Colorado, New Mexico, and Wyoming.

Polk made other efforts to expand the United States. He offered Spain $100 million for Cuba. But Spain turned down the offer. Polk chose not to run for a second term and died only three months after he left office.

Map of acquired territory of the United States from 1492 to Polk's time.

CLAIMED BY THE UNITED STATES. DISCOVERY, 1792. LOUISIANA PURCHASE. EXPLORATION, 1805. SETTLEMENT, 1811.

NDARY LINE AS ADJUSTED

LOUISIANA PURCHASE 1803.

NORTH-WEST TERRITORY, 1787.

FIRST MEXICAN CESSION, 1848.

ORIGINAL AREA OF THE UNITED STATES.

TREATY WITH.

CEDED TO THE U.S. BY TEXAS IN 1850.

ACQUIRED BY ANNEXATION 1845.

SPAIN IN 1819.

GADSDEN PURCHASE 1853

SPANISH CESSION 1819.

ALASKA PURCHASED FROM RUSSIA 1867.

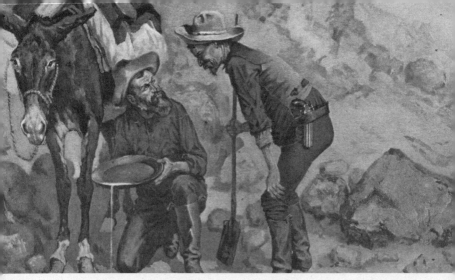

A painting of two prospectors panning for gold by Frederic Remington. Gold was discovered in California in January 1848. By 1849, 80,000 prospectors were pouring into the "Golden State."

JAMES POLK
Important Events

1845 – Texas admitted as the 28th state

1846 – Iowa admitted as the 29th state

1846 – U.S. declared war on Mexico

1846 – Treaty concluded with Great Britain establishing Oregon boundary

1848 – Gold discovered in California

1848 – Wisconsin admitted as the 30th state

ZACHARY TAYLOR

12th President

Born: November 24, 1784

Birthplace: Montebello, Orange County, Virginia

Previous experience: Military leader

Political party: Whig

Term of office: March 4, 1849– July 9, 1850

Died: July 9, 1850

Zachary Taylor was the first military leader to become president without first holding other government posts. His father had been a colonel in the Revolution, and talk of battles flowed through the Taylor home.

At the age of 18, Taylor had a commission in the army; he remained a soldier for the next forty years. He fought in the War of 1812 and in the Mexican War of 1846, and he fought against the Seminole Indians in Florida.

The Mexican War made Taylor a national hero. As the leader of 5,000 American volunteers, he defeated Santa Anna and a force nearly four times larger than his own.

Taylor did not look like a military hero. He was a squat little man who had to be boosted into his saddle. "Old Rough and Ready" preferred wearing the simple clothes of a farmer rather than a military uniform.

Taylor had little interest in politics. But the Whigs nominated him anyway—and he won. At the White House, he strolled about, shaking hands with anyone who stopped by.

HE LET HIS OLD WAR HORSE GRAZE ON THE WHITE HOUSE LAWN.

Although he was a slave owner, Taylor didn't want to see slavery extended into the territories won in the Mexican War. He also wanted New Mexico and California added to the Union as free—not slave—states.

Zachary Taylor was not president for very long. On the Fourth of July, 1850, sixteen months after taking office, he took part in ceremonies at the then-unfinished Washington Monument. The day was broiling hot. Taylor suffered a sunstroke and died five days later.

ZACHARY TAYLOR
Important Event

1850 - Clay Compromise passed, providing for the admission of California as a free state and the formation of the territories of New Mexico and Utah

MILLARD FILLMORE

13th President

Born: January 7, 1800

Birthplace: Summerhill, New York

Previous experience: Lawyer, congressman, vice president

Political party: Whig

Term of office: July 10, 1850– March 3, 1853

Died: March 8, 1874

The day after President Zachary Taylor's death, his vice president, tall, handsome Millard Fillmore, took the oath of office.

Millard Fillmore was the son of a poor New York farmer. As a small boy, he helped his father clear land and raise crops. Then he was sent away to learn the clothmaker's trade. His master treated him so harshly that Millard borrowed $30 to purchase his freedom, then hiked over 100 miles back to his log-cabin home.

Millard was 18 when he attended his first school. He fell in love with his schoolteacher, Abigail Powers. Seven years later, she became his wife.

At 23, Fillmore got a job as a law clerk and went on to become a lawyer. He was elected to the New York State Assembly and then became a U.S. congressman. At the Whig Convention in 1848, when he was 48, Fillmore was chosen as the party's vice-presidential candidate.

The White House in President Fillmore's day.

During his term as president, Fillmore modernized the White House. A cast-iron stove replaced the huge fireplace that had been used for cooking.

PLUMBERS PUT IN THE FIRST WHITE HOUSE BATHTUB WITH RUNNING WATER.

When Abigail Fillmore set aside a White House room for a library, Congress granted her $250 to buy books.

President Fillmore saw the slavery issue grow dangerously hot. In the North, many people wanted to end slavery, while many Southerners wanted to see slavery spread to the new Western states. Fillmore himself didn't have strong opinions on slavery. Then Congress passed the Fugitive Slave Act, making federal officials responsible for returning runaway slaves to their Southern masters. Fillmore could kill the bill by refusing to sign it, or make it law by putting his signature on it. Fillmore signed.

This turned out to be a big mistake. Antislavery Northerners hated the new law. Mobs attacked federal marshals to free slaves they had captured.

The North never forgave Fillmore or the Whig Party, which died away.

MILLARD FILLMORE
Important Events

1850 – California admitted as the 31st state

1850 – Fugitive Slave Act became law

1853 – Washington Territory created out of northern half of Oregon

FRANKLIN PIERCE

14th President

Born: November 23, 1804

Birthplace: Hillsborough, New Hampshire

Previous experience: Lawyer, congressman, senator

Political party: Democrat

Term of office: March 4, 1853– March 3, 1857

Died: October 8, 1869

Franklin Pierce was among our youngest presidents; he was only 48 when he was elected. Like President Fillmore, Pierce was a Northerner who was "soft" toward the South on slave issues. These men were called "doughfaces" because their opinions could be kneaded like dough by pro-slavery Southerners.

Young Franklin was educated in private schools and entered college at 15. At Bowdoin College, Maine, his classmates included the famous writers Nathaniel Hawthorne and Henry Wadsworth Longfellow.

After he graduated, Pierce studied law and went into politics, holding various state offices. He was elected to Congress, and in 1836, at the age of 32, he became the youngest senator in Washington.

Pierce did not seek the presidency. His friends put his name in nomination when the Democratic convention became deadlocked.

Although he made no campaign speeches, he won the election easily, defeating General Winfield Scott and the dying Whig party.

Pierce was handsome and fun-loving. But his life was scarred by tragedy. Two of his sons died in infancy. A third son, Benjamin, was 11 years old at the time Pierce was elected president. Just before his inauguration, Pierce, his wife, and son were traveling by train from Boston to Concord, New Hampshire, when their railroad car was derailed and overturned. Pierce and his wife were slightly injured, but young Benjamin was crushed to death.

PIERCE'S TERM AS PRESIDENT WAS TINGED WITH TRAGEDY, TOO.

He helped to get the Kansas-Nebraska Act passed. It allowed new settlers there to vote whether or not to have slavery, and that led to bloody fighting between the proslavery and antislavery groups—a foretaste of the Civil War.

A political cartoon depicting Pierce in the "Great Footrace for the Presidential Purse" by N. Currier.

An engraving of Franklin Pierce on horseback by W. L. Ormsby.

At the Democratic National Convention in 1856, Pierce was rejected by his party in favor of James Buchanan, who was more neutral on the slavery question. Pierce returned to his New Hampshire home in bitterness.

FRANKLIN PIERCE
Important Events

1854 – Kansas-Nebraska Act passed, permitting state residents to decide slavery issue

1854 – U.S. acquired border territories from Mexico through Gadsden Purchase

15th President

Born: April 23, 1791

Birthplace: Cove Gap, Pennsylvania

Previous experience: Lawyer, congressman, senator, diplomat, **cabinet member**

Political party: Democrat

Term of office: March 4, 1857– March 3, 1861

Died: June 1, 1868

By the time James Buchanan became president, at 65, the nation was facing war over slavery. "Old Buck" had had 43 years of shining government experience, but it didn't help him in grappling with the grave problems of the day. He was old and tired and too cautious by nature to make hard decisions.

Buchanan was the oldest of eleven children. Born in a Pennsylvania log cabin, he learned arithmetic by helping out in his father's store. At 18 he graduated from Dickinson College, and before he was 30, he had made $300,000.

Buchanan studied law and built a very successful law practice. He was not so successful in love. Shortly after his bride-to-be broke their engagement over a misunderstanding, she died, and the heartbroken Buchanan never married. He turned, instead, to public service. He was a congressman for ten years and a senator for twelve years.

Under presidents Jackson, Polk, and Pierce, Buchanan was a top-level foreign diplomat.

By serving in foreign countries, Buchanan had avoided the bitter arguments about slavery, and this helped him win the nomination at the Democratic National Convention in 1856.

Shortly after Buchanan became president, the Supreme Court handed down the fateful Dred Scott decision. Basically, it said that Congress had no power to interfere with slavery. Northerners were furious and fought against the ruling.

But Buchanan refused to take sides.

"YOU ARE SLEEPING ON A VOLCANO," HE WAS WARNED.

The slave-owning Southern states threatened to secede—that is, to leave the United States and form their own country—unless slavery

An engraving of Dred Scott and his wife Harriet from Frank Leslie's Illustrated Newspaper. The Dred Scott decision meant that slave hunters could search for runaway slaves and take them from free states.

An old plantation home in Mississippi. Many slaves in Maryland and Virginia were "sold down the river" to cotton plantation owners in the Deep South.

was protected. Buchanan said that a state had no right to secede, but that, on the other hand, the federal government had no legal right to stop a state from seceding.

In Buchanan's last months as president, South Carolina did secede, soon followed by six other states. They set up the Confederate States of America under Jefferson Davis. Still Buchanan did nothing.

Rejected by both sides, Buchanan left the White House in 1861. With great relief he handed over the reins of government to his successor, Abraham Lincoln, and slipped away to his Pennsylvania home.

JAMES BUCHANAN
Important Events

1857 – Dred Scott decision announced by Supreme Court

1858 – Minnesota admitted as the 32nd state

1858 – Atlantic cable completed

1859 – Oregon admitted as the 33rd state

1860 – Pony Express service began between St. Joseph, Missouri, and Sacramento, California

1860 – South Carolina seceded from the Union

1861 – Kansas admitted as the 34th state

1861 – Confederate States of America organized

FUN FACT:
JAMES BUCHANAN, INAUGURATED IN 1857,
IS THE ONLY PRESIDENT WHO NEVER MARRIED.

ABRAHAM LINCOLN

16th President

Born: February 12, 1809

Birthplace: Hardin County, Kentucky

Previous experience: Lawyer, congressman

Political party: Republican

Term of office: March 4, 1861– April 15, 1865

Died: April 15, 1865

Abraham Lincoln led the fight to save the Union and end slavery. Although he had only a scant frontier education and little experience in public office, his keen judgment and deep sense of humanity made him one of our greatest presidents.

Abraham Lincoln was born in a dirt-floor log cabin. The Lincoln family was always poor. His father, a carpenter, never learned to read or write.

When Abe was almost eight, the Lincolns moved to Indiana. Less than two years later, his mother, Nancy Hanks, died of the "milk sickness," leaving Abe and his older sister, Sarah. His father remarried and Sarah Johnson became the new Mrs. Lincoln. A widow with three children of her own, she brought warmth to the family and encouraged young Abe to better himself. He called her his "best friend in this world."

At 16, Abe was tall, slim, and strong. He did odd jobs for anyone who would hire him. He worked as a farmhand, grocery clerk, and rail splitter, reading and studying whenever he could.

He also worked as a deckhand on a flatboat that floated down the Ohio and Mississippi rivers to New Orleans. On one such trip he saw chained blacks being whipped and beaten.

HE HATED SLAVERY FROM THAT DAY.

Lincoln received his license to practice law in 1836 and began "traveling the circuit." He and other lawyers would ride on horseback from village to village, trying cases. The work sharpened his skills as a debater.

Lincoln was elected to Congress as a Whig in 1847. Then he quit politics and returned to Springfield, Illinois, to practice law again, becoming one of the best-known lawyers in Illinois. He was in his early forties now, married to Mary Todd, and the father of four sons.

Lincoln turned his attention to politics a second time in 1855, speaking out against the Kansas-Nebraska Act that said people in the Western territories could have slavery if they voted for it.

Illinois Senator Stephen A. Douglas was the author of this act. In 1858 Lincoln left the Whigs to join the antislavery Republican Party. He wanted to run against Douglas for the Senate. Lincoln challenged Douglas to a series of debates. Although Lincoln lost the election, the debates made him nationally famous; he was nominated for the presidency in 1860.

Within six weeks after Lincoln had taken office as president, Southern troops attacked Fort Sumter in the harbor of Charleston, South Carolina. They shot down the flag and captured the fort. The next day Lincoln issued a call for 75,000 volunteers to retake the fort and other property now in Confederate hands. This was the start of the Civil War.

Lincoln was president throughout the war's four bitter years. In mid-1862 he issued his famous Emancipation Proclamation, which gave freedom to some three million blacks in the South.

Northern forces suffered one battlefield defeat after another in the early stages of the war. But in 1863 and 1864, the tide began to turn in the Union's favor. Lincoln was reelected in 1864.

When he took the oath of office, the war's end was in sight.

LINCOLN URGED THAT, INSTEAD OF TAKING VENGEANCE AGAINST THE SOUTH, THERE BE "MALICE TOWARD NONE" AND "CHARITY FOR ALL."

Lincoln, at the battlefront, talks with Union Army officers.

A lithograph of the assasination of President Lincoln, originally published by Currier & Ives.

Tragically, Lincoln had no opportunity to put his postwar policies into effect. On April 14, 1865, five days after the surrender of Confederate forces, Lincoln was attending the theater with his wife, when a man named John Wilkes Booth crept up from behind and shot him in the head. The president died the next day. Speaking for the sorrowing nation, one cabinet member said, "now he belongs to the ages."

ABRAHAM LINCOLN
Important Events

1861 – First attack in Civil War at Fort Sumter, South Carolina

1862 – Battle between the *Monitor* and the *Merrimac*

1862 – Emancipation Proclamation issued

1863 – West Virginia admitted as the 35th state

1864 – Nevada admitted as the 36th state

1865 – General Robert E. Lee surrendered to General
Ulysses S. Grant, ending Civil War

FUN FACT:
AT CLOSE TO 6 FEET 4 INCHES, ABRAHAM LINCOLN IS THE
TALLEST PRESIDENT. HE WEIGHED ABOUT 180 POUNDS.

17th President

Born: December 29, 1808

Birthplace: Raleigh, North Carolina

Previous experience: Tailor, congressman, governor, senator

Political party: Democrat

Term of office: April 15, 1865– March 3, 1869

Died: July 31, 1875

With the death of President Lincoln, the presidency fell to Andrew Johnson, a southern Democrat whom Lincoln had picked to be his vice president in 1864. A convincing speaker, Andrew Johnson was largely self-taught. His parents had been too poor to send him to school. He learned to read and write while he was serving as apprentice to a tailor.

Later, Johnson set up as a tailor in Greeneville, Tennessee, and took part in debates at the local school. He married and became mayor of the town, then a congressman. He was elected governor of Tennessee, and then at 49, he became a U.S. senator.

Although a Southerner, Johnson was loyal to the Union cause and opposed secession. The other Southern senators branded him a traitor.

WHEN THE CIVIL WAR BROKE OUT, EVERY SOUTHERN SENATOR QUIT AND WENT BACK HOME – EXCEPT ANDREW JOHNSON.

In 1862 President Lincoln appointed Johnson military governor of Tennessee. And two years later, impressed by Johnson's moderate views, Lincoln chose him as his vice president.

Now President Johnson proceeded to "reconstruct" the ex-Confederate states while Congress was not in session. Many Northern members of Congress wanted to punish the Southerners as rebels and traitors. But Johnson pardoned all who would take an oath of allegiance. The struggle became more bitter as Congress passed bills over Johnson's veto.

Finally, when Johnson dismissed Secretary of War Stanton from his cabinet without the permission of Congress, Congress acted to impeach him. Johnson went on trial, accused of "high crimes and misdemeanors."

The trial lasted two months. The House voted for impeachment, but

An engraving of the impeachment trial of Andrew Johnson by artist Theodore R. Davis.

the Senate was a single vote short of the two-thirds majority needed to remove a president from office. Johnson finished his term.

Johnson actually sought the presidential nomination again in 1868, but his party rejected him.

Finally, in 1874, he was elected to his old office as U.S. senator from Tennessee. When he took his Senate seat, Johnson was loudly applauded in the very chamber where he had been tried only seven years before.

ANDREW JOHNSON
Important Events

1865 – Thirteenth Amendment to the Constitution ratified, abolishing slavery

1867 – Nebraska admitted as the 37th state

1867 – Secretary of State William H. Seward arranged to buy Alaska from Russia

1868 – Fourteenth Amendment to the Constitution ratified, establishing rights of citizens

FUN FACT:
ANDREW JOHNSON, WHO WAS A TAILOR BEFORE HE BECAME PRESIDENT, WOULD ONLY WEAR SUITS THAT HE HIMSELF HAD MADE.

ULYSSES SIMPSON GRANT

18th President

Born: April 27, 1822

Birthplace: Point Pleasant, Ohio

Previous experience: Military leader

Political party: Republican

Term of office: March 4, 1869–March 3, 1877

Died: July 23, 1885

At the beginning of the Civil War, Hiram (his given name) Ulysses Grant was an unknown clerk in his father's store. By the end of the war, as Ulysses Simpson Grant, he was the nation's most celebrated general. (The name Simpson was acquired through an accidental change.)

The son of a farmer and tanner, young "Lyss" disliked both farming and tannery work. Horses were what he liked, and he rode like a champion.

Although his schooling had been irregular, it was enough to get Grant into the U.S. Military Academy at West Point, from which he graduated. In the Mexican War, Grant fought under General Zachary Taylor. He was cited for bravery and promoted to the rank of captain.

After the Mexican War, Grant found that his low army pay was not enough to support his wife and family, so he resigned.

77

He tried farming, then sold real estate, and when that too failed, he went to work in his brother's leather shop.

Then came the Civil War, and Grant rejoined the army. In the East, the war was going badly for the Union forces, but in the West, Grant began winning victories, one after another.

This led President Lincoln to put him in command of the entire Union army, and Grant led the North to victory. It was spring when the Southern forces surrendered, and Grant let the Southern soldiers keep their horses so that they could do their spring plowing.

Grant was a national hero after the war. The Republicans picked him to run for president, and he won easily.

Grant and his family.

A rare, informal photo of Grant, the soldier.

AS PRESIDENT, GRANT MADE ERRORS OF JUDGMENT THAT LOST HIM THE NATION'S RESPECT.

He appointed friends to high positions in the government; when they cheated, stole, and took bribes, the easygoing president got the blame.

After he left the presidency, Grant put his life savings into a banking firm. But his partner was a crook, and Grant lost all his money.

When Grant learned he was suffering from throat cancer, he courageously began to write his life story so that his wife would have money to live on. The book made the family rich. But Grant never knew that. Four days after he wrote the last word, he died.

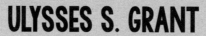

ULYSSES S. GRANT
Important Events

1869 – First transcontinental railroad service

1876 – Alexander Graham Bell transmitted the sound of human voice on the telephone

1876 – General George Custer's forces destroyed by Indians led by Sitting Bull at Little Big Horn, Montana

1876 – Colorado admitted as the 38th state

RUTHERFORD BIRCHARD HAYES

19th President

Born: October 4, 1822

Birthplace: Delaware, Ohio

Previous experience: Lawyer, military leader, congressman, governor

Political party: Republican

Term of office: March 4, 1877– March 3, 1881

Died: January 17, 1893

Although Rutherford B. Hayes nearly lost the election, he came to be respected by everyone as an honest, hardworking, and serious-minded president.

Hayes's father died before he was born, and he was raised by an uncle, who saw that young "Rud" got a good education. Hayes was a successful criminal lawyer in Cincinnati for several years, then fought in the Civil War, becoming a brevet major general in the Union Army.

Hayes was still at the front when he was elected to Congress. He later served two terms as governor of Ohio, and then the Republicans picked him to run for president.

The election was so close that everyone, even Hayes, thought he had lost to Tilden, the Democratic candidate. Hayes's backers challenged returns from three Southern states, and Congress established an Electoral Commission to investigate. It was finally decided, shortly before Inauguration Day, that Hayes, not Tilden, had been elected president.

A print of Hayes and his cabinet members, published by Currier & Ives.

In the White House, Hayes's wife, the former Lucy Webb, was known as "Lemonade Lucy" because she would not permit alcoholic beverages to be served. She would not allow card playing or dancing, and wore high-necked gowns for evening wear. Even so, social functions at the White House were popular and well attended. The Hayeses were friendly and hospitable and often the reception rooms served as "bedrooms" for overnight guests.

Hayes pledged protection of African-American rights, but he removed the last federal troops from the South to encourage self-government. From then on, the Southern states have typically voted as the "Solid South." Hayes insisted that appointments to government jobs should go to the best-qualified people.

DURING HAYES'S TERM, ONE OF THE FIRST TELEPHONES WAS INSTALLED IN THE WHITE HOUSE.

The inventor, Alexander Graham Bell, gave the president a personal demonstration. Thomas Edison was also a White House guest. He showed Hayes another of his inventions, the phonograph.

Hayes refused to run for a second term. He lived quietly in retirement at his home in Fremont, Ohio, until his death in 1893.

Thomas Alva Edison developed the phonograph and invented the incandescent electric light bulb.

RUTHERFORD B. HAYES
Important Events

1878 – Thomas Edison obtained patent for the phonograph

1879 – Edison invented the first electric incandescent lamp

1880 – New York City cited as the first U.S. city with a population of over one million

20th President

Born: November 19, 1831

Birthplace: Orange, Ohio

Previous experience: Teacher, military leader, congressman, senator

Political party: Republican

Term of office: March 4, 1881– September 19, 1881

Died: September 19, 1881

James A. Garfield was the last president to be born in a log cabin. James lost his father when he was only two years old. He worked hard as a boy, cutting wood, planting and reaping, and going to school whenever time allowed. When he was 16, he worked as a "tow boy," driving the horses and mules that pulled the boats on the Ohio Canal.

Garfield managed to graduate from college, working part of his way as a janitor, and became a professor of classics (Greek and Latin).

SINCE HE COULD WRITE WITH EITHER HAND, HE LIKED TO AMUSE PEOPLE BY WRITING GREEK WITH ONE HAND AND LATIN WITH THE OTHER—AT THE SAME TIME!

When President Lincoln called for volunteers in 1861, Garfield joined up and showed unusual bravery. Even though his horse was shot from under him, Garfield delivered a message that saved his regiment from disaster. For that, he won a battlefield promotion to major general.

Garfield served as a member of Congress for 18 years. He became a recognized leader of his party and was made a U.S. senator in 1880.

That was a presidential election year, and the Republicans could not decide on a candidate. They voted 35 times without coming to a decision. On the next ballot, they nominated Garfield, who won the election.

At this time in the 1880s, civil service jobs were not granted by taking merit exams. Instead, government jobs were often handed

Garfield with his family.

out to friends or political cronies by those in power. After Garfield's inauguration, office seekers swarmed into the White House. People even stopped the president's carriage on the street to ask him for jobs.

The president could not give a job to everyone who asked. Among those he had to disappoint was a man named Charles Guiteau.

Less than four months after he had taken office, Garfield was waiting for a train at the station in Washington. Guiteau stepped forward and fired two shots, and Garfield slumped to the floor.

The wounded president was carried to the White House. Doctors were unable to locate and remove the bullets. (X-rays would not be invented for another 14 years.) Just 80 days after he was shot, Garfield died.

JAMES GARFIELD
Important Event

1881 – American Red Cross organized

CHESTER ALAN ARTHUR

21st President

Born: October 5, 1830

Birthplace: Fairfield, Vermont

Previous experience: Public official, vice president

Political party: Republican

Term of office: September 20, 1881– March 3, 1885

Died: November 18, 1886

Garfield's assassination made Vice President Chester Alan Arthur the nation's leader. Many people were afraid that he would do whatever the politicians told him to do. But Arthur surprised his critics with his honesty and courage.

A tall, handsome man, Arthur had become wealthy as a lawyer in New York City and lived very well. He had a French cook and often spent two hours having dinner. He dressed elegantly in the latest fashions.

AFTER BECOMING PRESIDENT, ARTHUR SAID THE WHITE HOUSE WAS TOO GLOOMY FOR HIM.

He refused to live in the executive mansion until it suited his tastes. To make way for the expensive new furniture he ordered, 24 wagonloads of old things had to be carted away.

A political cartoon originally published by Keppler & Schwarzmann, showing Chester A. Arthur as a magician, pulling out cards labeled with different government jobs.

Arthur's political cronies were jubilant when he became president. They expected him to hand out jobs to his friends, as many politicians did at this time.

But Arthur showed he had a mind of his own. He worked to bring about a fair system of filling government jobs and persuaded Congress to pass the nation's first "bipartisan" civil service law. By this law, job seekers had to pass tests to get certain types of government jobs, and they could not be removed from their jobs for political reasons.

Arthur also worked to modernize the navy. He got new ships built to replace those that dated back to the Civil War.

Arthur would have liked to have run for the presidency in 1884. But although his good record pleased the people of the country, he had not pleased the leaders of the Republican party. He was not considered as a candidate in 1884. Arthur's courage cost him his career in politics. He returned to his wealthy law practice in New York City for two more years.

CHESTER ARTHUR
Important Events

1883 – Civil Service Commission organized

1884 – Territorial government in Alaska established

1885 – Washington Monument dedicated

FUN FACT:
MORE PRESIDENTIAL BIRTHDAYS OCCUR IN OCTOBER, LIKE ARTHUR'S, THAN IN ANY OTHER MONTH. THERE ARE SIX OF THEM.

22nd and 24th President

Born: March 18, 1837

Birthplace: Caldwell, New Jersey

Previous experience: Lawyer, sheriff, mayor, governor

Political party: Democrat

Terms of office: March 4, 1885–March 3, 1889 (first term); March 4, 1893–March 3, 1897 (second term)

Died: June 24, 1908

Grover Cleveland served one term as president, and then later served a second term. He was the only president ever to do this.

Cleveland was born in New Jersey, a preacher's son and one of nine children. He grew up in upstate New York and became a lawyer. As sheriff of New York's Erie County, Cleveland exposed many dishonest people. Later, he ran on his reform record and was elected mayor of Buffalo and then governor of New York state. He truly believed: "A public office is a public trust."

Cleveland's simple honesty and willingness to say "no" to politicians earned him many enemies, but more friends. He swept to victory in 1884, the first Democratic president in 25 years.

Cleveland was one of the hardest-working presidents; he often stayed up until two o'clock in the morning, working on the nation's problems. He stood for old-fashioned honesty. He refused to grant Civil War pensions that seemed fraudulent, and he forced the railroad companies to give back 81 million acres of Western land.

Cleveland was also one of the largest presidents, weighing in at around 260 pounds.

YOUNG RELATIVES CALLED HIM "UNCLE JUMBO."

One of the most popular events of Cleveland's presidency was his White House marriage to 22-year-old Frances Folsom, the daughter of his former law partner. She softened the stern president's public image, but not enough to get Cleveland reelected in 1888. He lost to the Republican candidate, Benjamin Harrison.

Before leaving the White House, Mrs. Cleveland told her staff: "Take care of the furniture. . . . We'll be coming back in four years." They did!

An engraving of Grover Cleveland's marriage to Frances Folsom by T. de Thulstrup.

Cleveland's second four years as president were not as happy. A serious business depression set off the Panic of 1897. Banks and businesses failed by the hundreds, and millions of people were out of work. Cleveland maintained the gold reserve, but he never really solved the people's problems, like unemployment and small business failures.

Cleveland retired to his home in Princeton, New Jersey. He died in 1908.

HIS LAST REPORTED WORDS WERE: "I HAVE TRIED SO HARD TO DO RIGHT."

GROVER CLEVELAND
Important Events

1893 – Chicago World's Fair opened

1896 – Utah admitted as the 45th state

FUN FACT:
GROVER CLEVELAND ONCE SERVED AS SHERIFF OF ERIE COUNTY, NEW YORK. AS SUCH, HE WAS THE PERSON ASSIGNED TO HANG CRIMINALS WHO HAD BEEN CONDEMNED TO DEATH, MAKING HIM THE ONLY PRESIDENT WHO ONCE HAD THE JOB OF PUBLIC EXECUTIONER.

BENJAMIN HARRISON

23rd President

Born: August 20, 1833

Birthplace: North Bend, Ohio

Previous experience: Lawyer, military leader, senator

Political party: Republican

Term of office: March 4, 1889–March 3, 1893

Died: March 13, 1901

Benjamin Harrison was "born into politics." His father was a congressman from Ohio. His grandfather, "Old Tippecanoe," was William Henry Harrison, the ninth president of the United States. And his great-grandfather signed the Declaration of Independence.

Ben went to school in a log schoolhouse, then studied law and became a lawyer in Indianapolis, where he campaigned for the Republican party. He fought in the Civil War and then returned to his law practice.

As a public figure, Harrison was respected but not really liked. He seemed cold and unfriendly. Sometimes he kept visitors standing while he tapped his pencil, hoping they would take the hint and leave.

His reputation as an "iceberg" cost Harrison the election for the Indiana governorship in 1876, but he later made a successful bid for the U.S. Senate. This victory was his stepping-stone to the presidency.

As president, Harrison took pride in his foreign policy. He established the basis of the Pan American Union and tried to get Hawaii annexed. Otherwise, he preferred to go along with Congress in handling the problems of the day.

During Harrison's administration, six new states were admitted to the Union: North Dakota, South Dakota, Montana, Washington, Idaho, and Wyoming. At last, the Bureau of the Census could report that the country was settled from coast to coast.

There were technological advances, too. Harrison was president when electic lighting was first installed in the White House.

BUT HE NEVER TOUCHED A LIGHT SWITCH FOR FEAR OF BEING ELECTROCUTED.

He also happened to be the last president to keep a full beard.

When Harrison ran for reelection in 1892, he was defeated by Grover Cleveland, the man he had narrowly beaten for the presidency four years earlier.

A photo of Harrison.

An early model of the Stanley steamer, a car that ran on steam; the two bearded men are the Stanley twins, who invented the car (1897).

BENJAMIN HARRISON
Important Events

1889 – North Dakota, South Dakota, Montana, and Washington admitted as the 39th, 40th, 41st, and 42nd states

1889 – Representatives of North and South American countries met in Washington for the first Pan American Conference

1890 – Sherman Antitrust Act enacted

1890 – Idaho and Wyoming admitted as the 43rd and 44th states

25th President

Born: January 29, 1843

Birthplace: Niles, Ohio

Previous experience: Soldier, lawyer, congressman, governor

Political party: Republican

Term of office: March 4, 1897– September 14, 1901

Died: September 14, 1901

William McKinley was a kind, gentle man, as thoughtful of the men in his regiment during the Civil War as he was, later, of his invalid wife. One of our best-loved presidents, he was an unlikely target for an assassin's bullet.

McKinley had been a lawyer, a Civil War soldier, a leader in Congress, and the governor of his state for two terms before being nominated for president.

As a presidential candidate in 1896, McKinley faced the fiery, young William Jennings Bryan. Bryan traveled across the country making speeches. But McKinley did not want to leave his wife; he campaigned near his home. Promising prosperous times and a "full dinner pail," McKinley won the election easily.

During McKinley's first term in office, the Spanish-American War began, with the slogan "Remember the Maine," after the U.S. battleship *Maine* was blown up in Havana harbor. The war lasted four months.

Out of the peace settlement, the United States got Guam, Puerto Rico, and the Philippines.

McKinley defeated Bryan again in the election of 1900.

BUT HIS SECOND TERM ENDED TRAGICALLY.

The president was greeting people at the Pan-American Exposition of 1901 in Buffalo, New York, when a young man named Leon Czolgosz approached him. Czolgosz's right hand was wrapped in a handkerchief to conceal a gun. He fired two bullets into the president. McKinley died eight days later.

WILLIAM MCKINLEY
Important Events

1898 – Battleship *Maine* blown up in Havana harbor, and U.S. declared war on Spain

1898 – Hawaii acquired by the U.S.

1898 – Treaty of Paris, ending Spanish-American War, signed

1899 – Guam, Puerto Rico, the Philippines, and American Samoa acquired by the U.S.

THEODORE (TEDDY) ROOSEVELT

26th President

Born: October 27, 1858

Birthplace: New York, New York

Previous experience: Rancher, governor, assistant secretary of the navy, vice president

Political party: Republican

Term of office: September 14, 1901– March 3, 1909

Died: January 6, 1919

As a child Theodore Roosevelt was too sickly to go to school. He had asthma, and was near-sighted, thin, weak, and nervous. Who could have guessed he would grow up to be our most vigorous president?

Luckily for Teddy, his father was wealthy enough to build a gym on the second floor of their New York City home. There, young Ted pounded away at a punching bag, did chin-ups on an iron bar, and twirled Indian clubs.

In college Teddy took up boxing. Then he set out for the Dakota Territory to hunt buffalo and work on a cattle ranch as a cowboy.

Back in New York, Roosevelt served as a crimebusting police commissioner. He fired crooked cops and rounded up gangsters. "Teddy the Scorcher" became a New York hero.

President McKinley made Roosevelt assistant secretary of the navy. Roosevelt called for a strong fleet. "Build a battleship in every creek!" he said. When the Spanish-American War broke out, Roosevelt organized the Rough Riders cavalry unit and led them in a famous charge up Cuba's San Juan Hill. Now a popular hero, he was elected governor of New York.

Crooked politicians called Roosevelt a "wild man." They put him up as vice president to get him out of the way. Then McKinley was shot, and suddenly, Theodore Roosevelt was president.

AT 42, HE WAS THE YOUNGEST ONE EVER.

As president, Roosevelt pushed through the Panama Canal and opened a transpacific cable. He declared himself an enemy of the giant trusts—big companies that controlled such industries as steel and coal. He fought their power and enforced antitrust laws, believing the trusts might become more powerful than the government.

Roosevelt hard at work in his office.

Roosevelt was one of the first presidents to realize the importance of conserving our wilderness lands and natural resources. He added more than 125 million acres to the national forest system.

Roosevelt's six energetic children made news in the White House. The younger ones walked on stilts over the floors, slid down banisters, and took their pony upstairs in the elevator.

Roosevelt was elected to a full term in 1904. After he retired as president, he went to Africa on a long trip of hunting and exploration, and much later, explored the jungles of Brazil. But Roosevelt didn't like being on the political sidelines. In 1912 he ran for the presidency on the Progressive "Bull Moose" Party and lost. He died seven years later at his home in Oyster Bay, New York.

Roosevelt and his family.

Theodore Roosevelt, center, with Colonel Leonard Wood of the Rough Riders.

THEODORE ROOSEVELT
Important Events

1901 – First wireless signal received from Europe

1903 – Departments of Commerce and Labor created

1903 – Wright brothers' airplane flight at Kitty Hawk, North Carolina

1904 – Panama Canal Zone acquired by the U.S.

1906 – San Francisco earthquake

1907 – Oklahoma admitted as the 46th state

1907 – American battleships departed on "round-the-world" cruise

WILLIAM HOWARD TAFT

27th President

Born: September 15, 1857

Birthplace: Cincinnati, Ohio

Previous experience: Lawyer, judge, governor of the Philippines, secretary of war

Political party: Republican

Term of office: March 4, 1909– March 3, 1913

Died: March 8, 1930

"Taft is the most loveable personality I have ever known," said Theodore Roosevelt when he backed William Howard Taft for president.

Taft demonstrated personal qualities that Roosevelt greatly admired—a zest for life and good sportsmanship. Taft liked to laugh and have fun. He played a fast game of tennis, and he was a graceful dancer in spite of his size.

WHEN THE 1910 BASEBALL SEASON OPENED, HE TOSSED OUT THE FIRST BALL, A CUSTOM MANY PRESIDENTS HAVE FOLLOWED SINCE THEN.

Taft was a huge man. He stood 6 feet, 2 inches tall and weighed over 300 pounds. He ate steak for breakfast; when he was worried, he munched on salted almonds. At Yale University he played baseball and football. After graduation he became a lawyer and then a judge, like his father and grandfather before him.

In 1898, when the United States acquired the Philippines, President McKinley chose Taft to govern the islands. Taft made a good governor. He set up public schools and a court system in the Philippines, and helped establish hospitals and banks there.

After McKinley's assassination in 1901, President Theodore Roosevelt called Taft back to Washington to serve in his cabinet. Roosevelt then helped Taft win the presidential election of 1908.

Roosevelt admired Taft's personal qualities, but he felt that Taft granted too many favors to businesses. He quarreled with Taft over tariff issues and his record on conservation. In 1912 Taft ran for a second term, strongly opposed by Roosevelt and his Progressive Party. Both men lost to Woodrow Wilson, the Democratic candidate.

Leaving the White House did not make Taft unhappy. He called it "the lonesomest place in the world."

In 1921 President Harding appointed Taft Chief Justice of the U.S. Supreme Court. It was an assignment Taft liked much better than being president. He started each day at 5:15 in the morning and carried out his duties with great delight and enthusiasm.

Taft served as chief justice for nine years. He is the only American to have held both the highest executive and highest judicial office.

Taft addressing the American people.

WILLIAM TAFT
Important Events

1909 – Peary discovered the North Pole

1912 – New Mexico admitted as the 47th state

1912 – Arizona admitted as the 48th state

1913 – Parcel Post service begins

1913 – Sixteenth Amendment to the Constitution ratified, establishing the income tax

FUN FACT:

AT 332 POUNDS, WILLIAM HOWARD TAFT—"BIG BILL," AS HE WAS KNOWN—WAS THE HEAVIEST PRESIDENT. AFTER LEAVING THE PRESIDENCY, HE BECAME CHIEF JUSTICE OF THE UNITED STATES.

WOODROW WILSON

28th President

Born: December 28, 1856

Birthplace: Staunton, Virginia

Previous experience: Teacher, university president, governor

Political party: Democrat

Term of office: March 4, 1913– March 3, 1921

Died: February 3, 1924

B efore Woodrow Wilson was thrust into politics, he had spent over thirty years as a college student, professor, and university president.

The son of a minister and the grandson of a printer from Ireland, Wilson studied law, practiced it briefly, and then became a professor of law and political economy at Princeton University.

Wilson was strict with his students, yet he was named the most popular teacher there. In 1902 he was made president of the university.

Eight years later, when New Jersey's Democratic leaders were looking for a quiet, respectable candidate for governor of the state, they picked Wilson. Since he was inexperienced in real politics, they figured that he would do what he was told.

But Wilson surprised the politicians. He cleaned up the state and got rid of crooks in business and politics. He was so successful that the

Wilson pitching at baseball's opening day in 1916.

national Democratic party, seeking a reform candidate to stand up to strong opposition, nominated Wilson for president. In 1912 Wilson defeated the Republican candidate Taft, and also Theodore Roosevelt, who ran on the Progressive Party ticket.

As president, Wilson called for cuts in taxes on imported goods, stronger antitrust laws, and our present Federal Reserve monetary system. In 1914 World War I broke out in Europe. Wilson was reelected in 1916 with the slogan, "He kept us out of war."

But early in his new term, German submarines sank several U.S. ships. Wilson sent warnings and then declared war on Germany on April 6, 1917.

IT WAS TO BE "A WAR TO END ALL WARS."

Early in 1918 Wilson proposed peace; in November the armistice was signed, and Wilson went to Paris for the peace talks. He called for a "League of Nations." The League would be a meeting place where nations could settle their quarrels without going to war.

Wilson was awarded the Nobel Peace Prize, but back home the U.S. Senate turned down Wilson's League of Nations plan. Bitterly disappointed, he traveled about the country pleading for his plan; then he suffered a stroke and never fully recovered. He died three years after leaving the White House.

In the years following his death, Wilson was often hailed for his liberalism, a political belief that came to be prominent during the administrations of Franklin Roosevelt, Lyndon Johnson, and, most recently, Barack Obama. But in contemporary times, Wilson's legacy has been tarnished by charges that the 28th president was a racist who supported segregation in government workplaces, particularly in the U.S. Treasury and the Department of the Interior. In 2015, student protestors at Princeton University called for the removal of the former president's name from the Woodrow Wilson School of Public and International Affairs.

While there is no doubt that Wilson, in many instances, did favor a government that was sharply segregated, he is still known for his progressive reforms in other areas. He is also recognized for his international leadership and his idea for the League of Nations, which today lives on as the modern United Nations.

WOODROW WILSON
Important Events

1913 – Federal Reserve Act passed

1915 – New York to San Francisco telephone demonstrated

1915 – Liner *Lusitania* sunk by German submarine

1916 – Senate ratified treaty to purchase Danish West Indies (Virgin Islands)

1917 – U.S. declared war on Germany

1918 – Armistice signed, ending World War I

1920 – First meeting of League of Nations called

1920 – Nineteenth Amendment to the Constitution ratified, giving women the right to vote

1921 – First continental airmail flight from San Francisco to New York

FUN FACT:
WOODROW WILSON, WHO EARNED A DOCTORATE DEGREE IN POLITICAL SCIENCE FROM JOHNS HOPKINS UNIVERSITY, RANKS AS THE HIGHEST EDUCATED PRESIDENT.

WARREN GAMALIEL HARDING

29th President

Born: November 2, 1865

Birthplace: Corsica, Ohio

Previous experience: Editor, lieutenant governor, senator

Political party: Republican

Term of office: March 4, 1921– August 2, 1923

Died: August 2, 1923

I don't expect to be the best president, but I hope to be the best loved one," said Warren G. Harding. But even in that, he was doomed to disappointment.

Harding was born in 1865, seven months after the Civil War's end. At the age of 19, Harding and two friends borrowed $300 and bought a newspaper—the *Marion* (Ohio) *Star*. The paper became a big success, and through it Harding got to know Ohio's political leaders. They helped him become lieutenant governor of Ohio and, later, a U.S. senator.

Tall, handsome, and friendly, Harding was a very popular senator. He had a smile and a pleasant word for everyone. The Republicans picked him to run for president in 1920.

IN HIS CAMPAIGN, HARDING PROMISED A "RETURN TO NORMALCY."

Americans, weary of wartime restrictions, swept Harding into office.

All went well at first. Wartime controls were taken off, taxes slashed. But President Harding surrounded himself with friends he trusted— and shouldn't have. Big oil scandals broke. One cabinet member went to jail for taking bribes. Other officials were accused of stealing government funds.

Alarmed and feeling wronged, Harding set out on a speechmaking tour to present his side of the story to America. During the trip, he suffered a heart attack and died suddenly, without having cleared his name.

WARREN HARDING
Important Events

1922 – U.S., Japan, Italy, Great Britain, and France sign limitation agreement on naval armaments

1922 – First woman senator, Rebecca L. Felton of Georgia, appointed

1923 – First woman member of Congress, Ella Mae Nola of California, took office

JOHN CALVIN COOLIDGE

30th President

Born: July 4, 1872

Birthplace: Plymouth, Vermont

Previous experience: Lawyer, public official, governor, vice president

Political party: Republican

Term of office: August 3, 1923– March 3, 1929

Died: January 5, 1933

I f ever a man could cool down talk of bribes and scandal, it was Coolidge, the most thrifty of the presidents.

Calvin Coolidge never wasted words. "You must talk with me, Mr. Coolidge," a woman once pleaded. "I made a bet that I could get more than two words out of you." President Coolidge looked straight at her. "You lose," he said.

COOLIDGE WAS THE ONLY PRESIDENT TO BE BORN ON THE FOURTH OF JULY.

As a boy, he worked on the family farm in Vermont—taking the cows to pasture, planting crops, and doing various farm chores. After college he became a lawyer in Northampton, Massachusetts, where he met and married Grace Goodhue, who was a teacher of the deaf. He entered politics, and during the next twenty years, "Silent Cal," as he was called, served in nineteen different public offices.

During his term as governor of Massachusetts, the police officers of Boston went on strike. Coolidge called out the state guard to keep order, saying, "There is no right to strike against the public safety by anybody, anywhere, anytime." This strong stand made Coolidge well known all over the country. The next year, he was elected vice president.

Coolidge was at his father's farm in Vermont when he was notified that President Harding had died. He got up in the middle of the night, dressed in his best black suit, and took the oath of office on the family Bible, in the presence of his notary public father and a few witnesses.

THEN THE NEW PRESIDENT OF THE UNITED STATES WENT BACK TO BED.

A print from the Everett collection of Coolidge taking the oath of office in his home following the death of President Warren G. Harding.

Coolidge and his wife, Grace.

As president, Coolidge obeyed the prohibition law. He did not serve alcoholic drinks. It is said that White House guests were sometimes served plain ice water—in paper cups! Still, with charming Grace Coolidge as first lady, social functions at the White House were popular and well attended. Coolidge cleaned up the scandals and extravagances of the Harding administration and reduced the national debt.

A contented nation reelected Coolidge to a full term in 1924. But it was not a happy term for him. Early in the campaign, the Coolidges' 16-year-old son died of blood poisoning. "When he went," said Coolidge, "the power and the glory of the presidency went with him."

In 1927 the Republicans wanted Coolidge to be their candidate once more. He answered, "I do not choose to run for president in 1928." When he left the White House, Coolidge was more popular than ever. Everyone had survived the jazz age of the 1920s by "keeping cool with Coolidge."

Coolidge signing the bill for the Coolidge Dam.

CALVIN COOLIDGE
Important Events

1923–1924 – Teapot Dome oil scandal revealed

1924 – Regular transcontinental airmail service established

1926 – Liquid-fueled rocket flown

1926 – Richard E. Byrd and Floyd Bennett made first flight over North Pole

1927 – Charles Lindbergh completed first transatlantic solo flight

HERBERT CLARK HOOVER

31st President

Born: August 10, 1874

Birthplace: West Branch, Iowa

Previous experience: Engineer, overseas U.S. Food and Relief administrator, secretary of commerce

Political party: Republican

Term of office: March 4, 1929– March 3, 1933

Died: October 20, 1964

Herbert Hoover's personal story is one of rags to riches. He was an orphan who became a successful engineer and a millionaire by the age of 40. But the nation's story during his administration is one of riches to rags. Hoover faced a national depression that brought the United States almost to its knees.

The years of the Great Depression were the unluckiest of Hoover's long lifetime—which included four separate careers.

The son of an Iowa blacksmith, Hoover was born poor and was an orphan by the age of eight. Raised by an aunt and uncle in Oregon, he studied to become a geologist and mining engineer at Stanford University. There he met and married Lou Henry, a fellow geologist, who traveled with him. Hoover's mining surveys took him all over the world. He discovered rich gold and iron deposits in Australia and China and became China's chief mining engineer.

Hoover's second career began after World War I, when he supervised the distribution of food to many millions of starving war refugees in Belgium and France. He extended the aid to Soviet Russia, telling critics that starving people shall be fed, no matter their politics.

HOOVER SERVED WITHOUT PAY AND GAVE SOME OF HIS OWN FORTUNE TO THE CAUSE.

He was secretary of commerce under Harding and Coolidge, but it was his fame as an organizer and administrator that led to Hoover's third career—as president. He was elected in 1928 by an electoral vote of 444 to 87.

Hoover in the White House.

Hoover with Amelia Earhart, the first female aviator to fly solo across the Atlantic Ocean.

Then came the economic crash of 1929. Very soon, more than twelve million Americans were out of work, and banks and businesses were failing by the thousands. People expected a bold and decisive leader, but Hoover was cautious and traditional. He presented a program of public works and business financing to Congress, but he felt that aid—food and unemployment pay—should be at a local level. Congress and the nation waited for 1932 to elect a new president— Franklin Roosevelt.

Hoover later found a fourth career under President Truman. He supervised a huge European relief program to feed starving victims of World War II. He was also coordinator of a committee to reorganize the executive branch of government. Hoover was in his 90th year when he died in New York City in 1964.

HERBERT HOOVER
Important Events

1929 – Stock market selling panic preceded the Great Depression

1929 – Richard Byrd made South Pole flight

1932 – Amelia Earhart completed first transatlantic solo flight by a woman

1932–1933 – Congress proposed 20th Amendment to the Constitution: President's term of office to begin on January 20 (rather than March 4) (1932); ratification completed January 23 (1933)

FUN FACT:
BEFORE BECOMING PRESIDENT, HERBERT HOOVER LIVED AND WORKED IN CHINA AS A MINING ENGINEER. HE AND HIS WIFE BOTH LEARNED TO SPEAK MANDARIN CHINESE. LATER, IN THE WHITE HOUSE, HE AND HIS WIFE WOULD SPEAK TO EACH OTHER IN CHINESE WHEN THEY DIDN'T WANT OTHERS TO KNOW WHAT THEY WERE SAYING.

FRANKLIN DELANO ROOSEVELT

32nd President

Born: January 30, 1882

Birthplace: Hyde Park, New York

Previous experience: Public official, lawyer, governor

Political party: Democrat

Term of office: March 4, 1933– April 12, 1945

Died: April 12, 1945

Much was expected of Franklin Roosevelt when he entered the White House. "Happy Days Are Here Again" had been the Democrats' campaign song. But this was the worst depression in the nation's history. No community was without its failed businesses, closed banks, and bread lines of the unemployed. Gray despair cloaked the entire nation.

Roosevelt talked to the people by radio in "fireside chats." (There was no television then.) His words were soothing and confident. "This great nation will revive," he declared.

"THE ONLY THING WE HAVE TO FEAR IS FEAR ITSELF."

Americans everywhere took hope. They would fight the Depression; they would defeat it.

Roosevelt during one of his "fireside chats."

Roosevelt matched his words with action. He launched a bold reform program called the "New Deal." He said it was meant to help all America, but especially the "forgotten man"—anyone who was poor and discouraged.

He set up huge public-works programs to encourage business and consumer spending. He used public funds to create jobs for the unemployed, and provide food for the hungry and shelter for the homeless. Farms and banks were saved. "I am an old campaigner, and I love a good fight," Roosevelt once said. He tackled the Great Depression with a warrior's spirit. Later, he displayed that same spirit as he led the nation to victory in World War II against Hitler's Germany.

Roosevelt's courage and zest for combat may have come from his long struggle against a crippling disease. In 1921 he suffered an attack of poliomyelitis, which cost him the use of his legs. But he never gave in to the disease, learning to get about by using heavy leg braces, crutches, and a wheelchair. He also learned to delegate work. His wife, Eleanor, traveled and represented him in many groups and appearances, and kept him in touch. He drew on the knowledge of many bright, young economists and political figures.

Roosevelt was elected to a second term in 1936, a third term in 1940, and a fourth term in 1944.

NO OTHER PRESIDENT SERVED AS LONG, AND NO OTHER WILL.

(Read the Fun Fact on page 123 to find out why!)

His fourth term was in its first months when Roosevelt attended a summit meeting at Yalta with Prime Minister Winston Churchill of Great Britain, and the Russian leader, Joseph Stalin. Roosevelt returned from the conference weary and ill. He died at Warm Springs, Georgia, less than a month before the war ended in Europe.

Roosevelt's grandchildren, Little Sistie and "Buzzie" Dall, playing at the White House in 1933.

Roosevelt's wife, Eleanor, was the first presidential spouse to hold press conferences, write a syndicated newspaper column, and speak at a national convention.

FRANKLIN DELANO ROOSEVELT
Important Events

1933 – "Hundred Days" congressional session in which New Deal recovery measures enacted

1933 – Tennessee Valley Authority (TVA), Civilian Conservation Corps (CCC), National Recovery Administration (NRA), and Public Works Administration (PWA) created

1933 – Wiley Post made first solo world flight

1935 – Works Progress Administration (WPA) established

1935 – Social Security Act passed

1938 – National minimum wage enacted

1939 – Opening of New York World's Fair

1939 – Germany invaded Poland; Britain and France declared war on Germany; World War II began

1940 – Registration for Selective Service began

1941 – Japan attacked Pearl Harbor, Hawaii, Guam, and the Philippines; U.S. declared war against Japan; Germany and Italy declared war against the U.S.

1942 – First demonstration of self-sustained nuclear chain reaction, Chicago

1943 – Pay-as-you-go income tax bill signed

1944 – Allied invasion of Europe in Normandy, France

1945 – Churchill, Stalin, and Roosevelt confer at Yalta

FUN FACT:

FRANKLIN D. ROOSEVELT WAS THE FIRST AND ONLY PRESIDENT ELECTED TO A THIRD TERM (IN 1940). FOUR YEARS LATER, HE WAS ELECTED TO A FOURTH TERM. THAT'S NO LONGER POSSIBLE. IN 1951, THE 22ND AMENDMENT TO THE CONSTITUTION WAS ADOPTED, WHICH LIMITS PRESIDENTIAL SERVICE TO TWO CONSECUTIVE TERMS.

HARRY S. TRUMAN

33rd President

Born: May 8, 1884

Birthplace: Lamar, Missouri

Previous experience: Farmer, store owner, judge, senator, vice president

Political party: Democrat

Term of office: April 12, 1945–January 20, 1953

Died: December 26, 1972

I've got the most awful responsibility a man ever had. If you fellows ever pray, pray for me," Harry Truman told newspaper reporters when he became president. (Franklin Roosevelt had died in office on April 12, 1945.)

Although Germany surrendered on May 7, the U.S. was still fighting in the Pacific, and Truman had to decide whether the new atomic bomb should be used against Japan. It would probably end the war and thus save lives. But no one knew exactly what its effects would be.

FINALLY, TRUMAN GAVE THE ORDER. AN ATOMIC BOMB WAS DROPPED ON THE CITY OF HIROSHIMA.

Three days later, another one was dropped over Nagasaki. Japan surrendered six days after that, ending World War II on August 15, 1945.

The mushroom cloud created by the atomic bomb that the United States dropped over Nagasaki, Japan, on August 9, 1945.

Harry S. Truman was born on a farm and managed it for his father for a time. He couldn't go to West Point because of poor eyesight, so he joined the National Guard, instead, and went overseas in World War I.

After the war, Major Truman ran a men's clothing store for a while. Then he went into politics in Missouri. He was elected to the U.S. Senate in 1936, and his fine record there led to his nomination as vice president with Franklin Roosevelt in 1944.

The next year, when Truman became president, he faced heavy postwar problems. Much of Europe lay in ruin. Millions were homeless and starving. Under the Truman Doctrine and, later, the Marshall Plan, America poured massive aid into the war-torn countries.

President Truman (center) at the Berlin Conference with Clement Attlee and Joseph Stalin.

In 1948 the experts said that Truman had no chance of being reelected. But his blunt, no-nonsense manner appealed to the voters. "The buck stops here" was his slogan. Truman startled the experts and won the election.

To halt the spread of Communism, Truman supported foreign aid programs and entered into military alliances with Western European nations. When Communist North Korea invaded South Korea in 1950, the United Nations appealed for troops, and Truman sent a U.S. force to Korea.

Truman was often described as a "man of the people." He was a plain-spoken, small-sized man with a temper, but this "average man" became a strong, decisive president at a critical time in world history.

HARRY TRUMAN
Important Events

1945 – Germany surrendered, ending World War II in Europe

1945 – United Nations charter signed at San Francisco

1945 – First atomic bomb detonated at Alamogordo, New Mexico

1945 – U.S. dropped atomic bombs on Hiroshima and Nagasaki, forcing Japan to surrender

1947 – Congress approved the "Truman Doctrine," authorizing aid to Greece and Turkey

1948 – Soviet Russia began Berlin blockade; U.S. and Great Britain began airlifting food to West Berlin (ended 1949)

1948 – Congress authorized the Marshall Plan

1949 – North Atlantic Treaty (NATO) signed by twelve nations

1950 – First U.S. ground troops sent to Korea

1951 – The 22nd Amendment ratified. It stated that "no person shall be elected to the office of the president more than twice."

1952 – Puerto Rico became a U.S. commonwealth

1953 – Korean war ended

DWIGHT (IKE) DAVID EISENHOWER

34th President

Born: October 14, 1890

Birthplace: Denison, Texas

Previous experience: Military leader, college president

Political party: Republican

Term of office: January 20, 1953–January 20, 1961

Died: March 28, 1969

Dwight David Eisenhower was called "Ike" by his boyhood pals. It was a nickname that stuck. During his campaign for the presidency, crowds chanted, "We like Ike!" Even as president, people still spoke of him as Ike. They weren't being disrespectful. It was just the comfortable way they felt about this friendly man with the big grin.

Ike was two years old when his family moved from Texas to Abilene, Kansas, where he and his five brothers were raised. At Abilene High School, he starred in baseball and football, and worked in a dairy to save money for college.

Ike went to West Point, and for a while it looked as though he might become one of Army's great football stars. But he broke his knee, and the injury ended his football career. Later, he became a good golfer.

World War I was raging in Europe at the time Eisenhower graduated from West Point, but he never got into battle. Instead, he served as the commander of 6,000 men at a tank training center near Gettysburg, Pennsylvania. From 1935 to 1939, he was an assistant to General Douglas MacArthur in the Philippines.

With the beginning of World War II, Eisenhower's career took off. By 1942 he was commanding general of all of our military forces in Europe. A year later, President Roosevelt named him to direct the Allied invasion of France, the invasion that freed Europe of Hitler's control.

General "Ike" Eisenhower, Commander in Chief of the
Allied Expeditionary Force, reviewing American troops in England, in 1944.

Eisenhower with John F. Kennedy.

WITH VICTORY IN EUROPE, EISENHOWER WAS HAILED AS AMERICA'S NUMBER-ONE HERO.

Both the Democrats and Republicans asked him to be a presidential candidate in 1948. Ike refused. But in 1952 he agreed to run—as a Republican. That year and again in 1956, he defeated the Democratic candidate, Adlai Stevenson.

Although Ike had been a military leader for most of his life, as president he worked hard for peace. He traveled many thousands of miles on goodwill missions. In a swing through Asia, millions cheered him in New Delhi and Tehran.

Also in his role as a peacemaker, Ike settled the Korean War. To ease tensions with the Soviet Union, he held a "summit conference" with the Russian Premier, Nikita Khrushchev.

Ike left the White House in January 1961 at the age of 70. He retired to his farm at Gettysburg, Pennsylvania. He died in 1969 at a military hospital near Washington.

DWIGHT EISENHOWER
Important Events

1953 – Korean War ended with signing of armistice

1954 – First nuclear submarine, *Nautilus*, launched

1954 – Supreme Court declared racial segregation in schools unconstitutional

1957 – Eisenhower Doctrine bill signed, authorizing use of U.S. forces to assist Middle East nations threatened by Communist aggression

1957 – First underground nuclear explosion

1957 – Federal troops sent to Little Rock, Arkansas, to enforce integration of black students

1958 – First American satellite, *Explorer I*, launched

1958 – National Aeronautics and Space Administration (NASA) established

1959 – Alaska and Hawaii admitted as the 49th and 50th states

★ JOHN (JACK) FITZGERALD KENNEDY ★

35th President

Born: May 29, 1917

Birthplace: Brookline, Massachusetts

Previous experience: Congressman, senator, author

Political party: Democrat

Term of office: January 20, 1961– November 22, 1963

Died: November 22, 1963

When he took office, John F. Kennedy was 43, the youngest man ever elected president. With his boyish smile and unruly shock of brown hair, he looked even younger.

Jack Kennedy was the second oldest in a family of nine children. The father, Joseph P. Kennedy, had once served as ambassador to Great Britain. He was a millionaire many times over, but he wanted his children to be tough and competitive. Debates and competitive sports were a part of growing up a Kennedy. Young Jack was sent to exclusive private schools and attended Harvard University.

Although he enjoyed many advantages, Kennedy's success did not come easily. His back, injured in a sea battle during World War II, never stopped hurting him. The same year Jack was injured, his brother Joe was killed while piloting a plane over Belgium.

After the war Jack went home and won election to Congress and later to the Senate. At a friend's dinner party, he met Jacqueline Lee Bouvier. They were married in 1953, and later had three children, one of whom died in infancy.

Kennedy was easily reelected to the Senate in 1958. Two years later, he was the Democratic presidential choice, opposing Richard Nixon. These two men were the first candidates to debate on television; the youthful, confident, witty Kennedy easily outshone the solemn, older Nixon.

Kennedy brought new style and vigor to the presidency. In his inaugural address, he declared,

"ASK NOT WHAT YOUR COUNTRY CAN DO FOR YOU— ASK WHAT YOU CAN DO FOR YOUR COUNTRY."

He sponsored the Peace Corps and a space project to land a man on the moon. He and Jackie hosted many concerts and encouraged the arts.

Senator John F. Kennedy, still a boyish presidential candidate, with daughter Caroline and Jacqueline, his wife.

President Kennedy declaring his goal to land a man on the moon, with Vice President Lyndon B. Johnson (left) and Speaker of the House Sam T. Rayburn (right) behind him.

Kennedy could also be tough. In October 1962, the U.S. learned that the Russians had brought missiles into Cuba. Kennedy ordered a naval blockade of Cuba. After thirteen tense days, the Russians removed the missiles.

Historians cite the test ban treaty as Kennedy's chief accomplishment. Signed by the U.S., the Soviet Union, and Great Britain, the treaty banned nuclear testing in the earth's atmosphere.

Six weeks after signing the treaty, Kennedy went on a speechmaking trip to Texas. In Dallas, on November 22, 1963, while he was riding in a motorcade, Kennedy was shot in the head by an assassin concealed in a nearby building. Kennedy died a few minutes later. The youngest man ever elected president, he was also, at 46, the youngest president to die in office.

JOHN F. KENNEDY
Important Events

1961 – First live television press conference held

1961 – Peace Corps created

1961 – U.S. launched Bay of Pigs invasion on south coast of Cuba

1961 – First U.S. astronaut, Commander Alan Shepard, rocketed into space

1961 – East Germany closed border between East and West Berlin

1962 – Lieut. Col. John Glenn was first U.S. astronaut to orbit earth

1962 – Supreme Court declared public school prayer to be unconstitutional

1963 – More than 200,000 Americans participated in Civil Rights march, Washington, DC

FUN FACT:
THE KENNEDY FAMILY HAD A DEEP FONDNESS FOR PETS. DURING THEIR WHITE HOUSE YEARS, THE KENNEDY MENAGERIE INCLUDED SEVERAL DOGS, A CAT, THREE BIRDS, TWO HAMSTERS, A RABBIT, AND THREE PONIES.

LYNDON BAINES JOHNSON

36th President

Born: August 27, 1908

Birthplace: Stonewall, Texas

Previous experience: Rancher, public official, senator, vice president

Political party: Democrat

Term of office: November 22, 1963– January 20, 1969

Died: January 22, 1973

A s vice president and native Texan, Lyndon Baines Johnson— LBJ—went with President John Kennedy on the fatal trip to Texas. On November 22, 1963, less than two hours after Kennedy had been shot, Johnson took the oath of office as president on board a plane that would rush him back to Washington.

A tall, rangy man, Johnson was 55 at the time, with more than thirty years' experience in politics—twelve as a U.S. senator. He was a very hard worker, an arm twister, a man who could get things done. "Come now, let us reason together," he liked to say.

In his first months as president, Johnson displayed enormous skill in getting new laws passed. The Civil Rights Act of 1964, a major education bill, a new tax law, an antipoverty program, and a food-stamp plan were all adopted.

When Johnson ran for reelection in 1964, he won an overwhelming victory. He pressed Congress to pass his "Great Society" program.

Under its terms, every American could look forward to a good education, a comfortable and useful life, and an old age without worry.

JOHNSON MIGHT HAVE EARNED A HIGH RANKING AMONG AMERICAN PRESIDENTS WERE IT NOT FOR ONE THING—THE VIETNAM WAR.

He plunged the nation deeper and deeper into that tragic conflict. By the time he left office in 1969, close to a half million U.S. troops were in Vietnam, and angry war protestors were marching on Washington with bitter slogans and chants directed at LBJ.

On March 31, 1968, Lyndon Johnson announced he would not run for reelection. He slipped away to the place he loved best—his ranch on the Pedernales River in Texas. He died there in 1973.

President Johnson shaking hands with Dr. Martin Luther King Jr., as he hands him a pen during the signing of the Civil Rights Act, July 2, 1964.

LYNDON JOHNSON
Important Events

1964 – Civil Rights Act signed into law

1964 – Antipoverty legislation signed

1964 – "Great Society" program proposed in State of the Union message

1965 – First American combat troops arrived in Vietnam

1965 – *Early Bird*, world's first commercial satellite, launched

1965 – President signed Medicare and voting-rights bills

1965 – Department of Housing and Urban Affairs created

1966 – Artificial heart pump successfully implanted

1968 – Dr. Martin Luther King Jr. assassinated

1968 – Senator Robert F. Kennedy assassinated

RICHARD MILHOUS NIXON

37th President

Born: January 9, 1913

Birthplace: Yorba Linda, California

Previous experience: Lawyer, congressman, senator, vice president

Political party: Republican

Term of office: January 20, 1969– August 9, 1974

Died: April 22, 1994

Richard M. Nixon, acknowledged leader in foreign policy, was the first president ever to resign, and he resigned under a cloud.

He was born on a lemon farm in Yorba Linda, California, on the outskirts of Los Angeles. His ancestors were colonial settlers whose descendants kept moving west with the frontier. Nixon graduated from Whittier College in California and then studied law in the East.

In both high school and college, Nixon was a champion debater. "He could take any side and win," said his debating coach.

After serving in the U.S. Navy during World War II, Nixon returned home to California and was elected to Congress in 1946. With national attention focused on his anti-Communist campaigns, he won a seat in the Senate and was Eisenhower's vice-presidential running mate in 1952.

Running for president in 1960, Nixon was the loser to John F. Kennedy in four televised debates and in the race for president.

Two years later, after losing in a race for governor of California, Nixon turned his back on politics. He joined a New York law firm. Little was heard from him for several years.

Then in 1968 Nixon staged a surprising comeback. He launched a smooth-running campaign for the presidency and won in a close race against Vice President Hubert Humphrey. (President Johnson did not enter the race.)

Nixon's first term as president was a triumph. He withdrew U.S. troops from Vietnam, winding down a war that had deeply divided the nation. In visits to China and the Soviet Union, he championed the cause of long-lasting peace. In 1972 Nixon was reelected by one of the greatest margins in U.S. history.

BUT TROUBLE WAS BREWING. EVEN BEFORE THE ELECTION, THERE WAS TALK OF A MAJOR SCANDAL—WATERGATE.

Police arrested five men who had burglarized the headquarters of the Democratic National Committee in the Watergate building in Washington and had installed wiretapping devices. As a Senate investigating committee probed for the truth, people close to Nixon, and Nixon himself, tried to cover up their involvement in this crime. Finally, in 1974 the House Judiciary Committee recommended adoption of impeachment proceedings.

Some of Nixon's top assistants had by then been convicted of bribery, fraud, and the obstruction of justice and sent to prison.

Nixon himself resigned in disgrace on August 9, 1974. (He was later pardoned by President Ford.)

In the years that followed, Nixon kept active, writing books, conferring with world leaders, and commenting on international relations.

Nixon salutes the crowd upon his final departure from the White House after his resignation.

RICHARD NIXON
Important Events

1969 – Astronauts Neil Armstrong and Edwin "Buzz" Aldrin became the first to land on the moon

1970 – U.S. began major withdrawals of troops from Vietnam

1972 – President visited Russia and China; conferred with Chinese Premier Chou-En-lai in Peking

1972 – Justice Department announced FBI would investigate Watergate break-in

1973 – Vietnam cease-fire agreement announced

1973 – Vice President Spiro T. Agnew resigned, to be replaced by Gerald R. Ford

1974 – Supreme Court ruled that women must receive equal pay for equal work

1974 – Seven former presidential aides indicted in Watergate conspiracy and President Nixon resigned

FUN FACT:
RICHARD NIXON WAS THE FIRST PRESIDENT
TO VISIT ALL FIFTY STATES.

38th President

Born: July 14, 1913

Birthplace: Omaha, Nebraska

Previous experience: Congressman, vice president

Political party: Republican

Term of office: August 9, 1974– January 20, 1977

Died: December 26, 2006

When Gerald Ford advanced to the presidency, he was the first vice president not elected by the people to become president.

He was chosen by Richard Nixon to be vice president when Nixon's original vice president, Spiro Agnew, had to resign. The House of Representatives and the Senate approved Nixon's choice. Later, when Nixon himself left office, Ford moved into the White House.

A rugged looking, athletic man with a quick smile, Gerald Ford seemed to be just the person to restore the country's faith in the presidency. He was open, honest, and decent.

Ford was a midwesterner, born in Omaha, Nebraska, and raised in Grand Rapids, Michigan. During his high school and college years, Ford was a star football player. He graduated from the University of Michigan and Yale University Law School.

President Ford waves to a crowd from the sunroof of a car.

Ford's career as a lawyer was interrupted by World War II. Joining the navy, he served for almost four years in the South Pacific. He was elected to Congress in 1948 and was then reelected as a member of Congress twelve times.

Nixon picked Ford as his vice president in October 1973. After Nixon's resignation, the country turned to Ford with hope and relief.

A MONTH AFTER TAKING OFFICE, FORD GRANTED NIXON A "FULL, COMPLETE, AND ABSOLUTE PARDON" FOR THE CRIMES HE WAS SAID TO HAVE COMMITTED.

For doing this, Ford was sharply criticized.

Ford's popularity also dwindled because of fuel shortages, inflation, and increasing unemployment. In foreign affairs, he followed Nixon's policy of holding talks with the Russian and Chinese heads of state.

In the presidential election of 1976, Ford faced an uphill battle against Jimmy Carter, a Democrat from Georgia. They debated three times on national television. Ford slowly gained ground but still lost in a close election.

After he left the White House, Ford wrote his autobiography, established his presidential library at the University of Michigan, and gave hundreds of speeches, often expressing his views on important political events of the time. For fun, Ford liked to golf, swim, and ski.

Gerald Ford died in 2006 at the age of 93. He is remembered as someone who became president as a result of the resignation of President Richard Nixon and other exceptional events in U.S. history. During his term of office, Ford did much to renew the nation's confidence in the presidency and the government in general.

GERALD FORD
Important Events

1974 – President granted unconditional pardon to former President Nixon

1974 – Nelson Rockefeller sworn in as vice president

1975 – Construction of Alaskan oil pipeline started

1975 – U.S. involvement in Vietnam ended with helicopter evacuation of last remaining Americans

1976 – Bicentennial of United States of America, marking 200 years since Declaration of Independence was signed

JAMES (JIMMY) EARL CARTER, JR.

39th President

Born: October 1, 1924

Birthplace: Plains, Georgia

Previous experience: Engineer, naval officer, farmer, businessman, state senator, governor

Political party: Democrat

Term of office: January 20, 1977– January 20, 1981

Died: —

A dark horse candidate who often spoke of himself as a "simple country boy," Jimmy Carter was the first southerner in more than a century to become president.

He grew up in the small town of Plains, Georgia (population 550), and took over the family's peanut business there when his father died. He was an active civic leader in his hometown, a school-board member, and a deacon of the local church. He married Rosalynn Smith, also from Georgia, and they had four children.

But the "simple country boy" also graduated with honors from the U.S. Naval Academy. He served in the navy's nuclear submarine program and studied nuclear physics. Returning home after resigning his naval commission, Carter became a state senator at 38, and governor of Georgia at 46.

He was serving as governor when he decided to run for president, even though he was practically unknown outside the South.

CARTER CRISSCROSSED THE NATION, PROMISING TO RESTORE TO THE PRESIDENCY "ALL THAT IS GOOD AND DECENT AND HONEST AND TRUTHFUL AND FAIR AND COMPETENT."

To Americans still reeling from the Watergate scandal, Carter's message had great appeal. At the Democratic convention in 1976, he was nominated on the first ballot and then won a narrow victory over Gerald Ford.

Carter worked hard as president to combat inflation and unemployment, but he failed to solve these problems. In foreign policy, he played a key role in bringing about a peace agreement between Israel and Egypt, but this bright success was overshadowed by a grim setback toward the final year of his term. Iranian students seized the U.S. embassy in Iran and held 52 Americans hostage. Americans were shocked and angry.

Negotiations for the release of the hostages dragged on for more than a year. Carter's popularity nose-dived. Freeing the hostages became an important campaign issue in 1980. Carter finally succeeded in obtaining their release on Inauguration Day, 1981, as the new President, Ronald Reagan, was taking office.

In the years since leaving office, Jimmy Carter has led an active life as a private citizen in a long string of diplomatic and humanitarian efforts. He participated in peace negotiations, monitored elections, and helped advance disease prevention in almost every part of the globe. As a result, many of Carter's most important accomplishments came after he left the White House.

Carter's struggles to advance human rights and reduce human suffering have been supported by the nonpartisan, nonprofit Carter Presidential Center in Atlanta, which the former president established

Egyptian President Anwar Sadat, President Carter, and Israeli Prime Minister Menachem Begin shake hands after signing the Mideast peace agreement in March 1979.

in 1982. The Center includes the Jimmy Carter Presidential Library and Museum.

His many accomplishments did not go unrecognized. In 2002, Carter was awarded the Nobel Peace Prize "for his decades of untiring effort to find peaceful solutions to international conflicts, to advance democracy and human rights, and to promote economic and social development."

Carter was a stern critic of both George W. Bush and Barack Obama. He condemned Bush for launching the war on Iraq and Obama for using drone strikes against suspected terrorists. Carter declared that the United States was no longer "the global champion of human rights."

In August 2015, Carter disclosed that cancer had been removed from his liver, but the disease had been discovered in his brain. Later that year, following treatment, Carter announced that he was cancer free.

"I'm perfectly at ease with whatever comes," Carter said, and then noted that he had led "a wonderful life.... Now I feel...it's in the hands of God."

JAMES (JIMMY) CARTER, JR.
Important Events

1977 – Established the U.S. Department of Energy

1979 – Established the U.S. Department of Education

1979 – Produced the first Middle East peace treaty between Israel and Egypt

1979 – U.S. officially recognized the People's Republic of China

1979 – Canal Zone ceded to Republic of Panama

1979 – U.S. Embassy personnel taken hostage in Iran

1980 – More than 125,000 refugees fled Cuba for the U.S.

1981 – Iran returned hostages to the U.S.

RONALD REAGAN

40th President

Born: February 6, 1911

Birthplace: Tampico, Illinois

Previous experience: Sports announcer, actor, union official, governor

Political party: Republican

Term of office: January 20, 1981– January 20, 1989

Died: June 5, 2004

At 69, Ronald Reagan was the oldest man ever elected President. But he seemed much younger, thanks to his vigorous and athletic appearance.

Ronald Reagan was born in Tampico, Illinois, the son of a shoe clerk whose income barely supported the family. His mother loved the theater, and from her, Ronald, or "Dutch" as he was called, developed an interest in acting.

In high school, Dutch appeared in several school plays, besides playing football and being captain of the swimming team. Later, he had leading roles in many college plays.

After graduation Reagan became a radio sports announcer. In 1937, when the Chicago Cubs went to spring training camp in California, Reagan went with the team to broadcast their games. While there, he made a screen test for a major motion picture studio, which led to an acting career.

Reagan was active with the Screen Actors Guild, a labor union of movie and television performers, serving for six years as president.

At the same time, Reagan was also active in national politics. He campaigned in 1948 for Harry Truman, a Democrat. But during the 1950s, as his views became more conservative, Reagan began supporting Republicans.

When someone suggested that he run for governor of California, Reagan laughed. He felt he didn't have a chance of winning. But when he tried in 1966, he defeated the Democratic candidate by a landslide. He was reelected governor in 1970 and served until 1975.

A year later, Reagan campaigned for the Republican presidential nomination. He lost to President Ford, who, in turn, lost the presidency to Jimmy Carter.

In 1980 Reagan tried for the Republican nomination again and won. President Carter, whose term had been dogged by issues he could not settle, was no match for Reagan. The former actor showed himself

Ronald Reagan and his wife, Nancy, campaining as governor.

President Reagan with the first woman justice of the Supreme Court, Sandra Day O'Connor, in 1981.

to be a skillful campaigner. He spoke firmly on issues, and, with his warm smile and easy, conversational style, he projected confidence. He won, hands down.

As president, Reagan defended basic values—work, the family, and patriotism. He slashed taxes, but also cut spending for welfare and unemployment programs.

HIS ECONOMIC POLICIES WERE CALLED "REAGANOMICS."

From the beginning, Reagan took a tough stand toward the Soviet Union. Even so, he held a series of conferences with Soviet leader Mikhail Gorbachev to shrink the nuclear arsenals of both nations. These meetings, along with reform programs launched by Gorbachev himself, helped to bring about an end to the long period of tension and conflict between the United States and the Soviet Union. That period was known as the Cold War.

In 1994, five years after leaving office, Reagan disclosed he had Alzheimer's disease. He died ten years later at the age of 93. Among former U.S. presidents, Ronald Reagan is always highly ranked in terms of popularity.

RONALD REAGAN
Important Events

1981 – Sandra Day O'Connor became first woman justice of the U.S. Supreme Court

1982 – First permanent artificial heart implanted

1983 – Peacekeeping force of U.S. Marines assigned to Lebanon (withdrawn, 1984)

1983 – U.S. troops invaded Grenada and ousted Cuban forces

1986 – Space shuttle *Challenger* exploded, killing the seven astronauts inside

1987 – President met with Soviet leader Mikhail Gorbachev in Washington and signed a nuclear missile treaty

GEORGE HERBERT WALKER BUSH

41st President

Born: June 12, 1924

Birthplace: Milton, Massachusetts

Previous experience: vice president, congressman, ambassador, Chairman of the Republican National Committee, Director of the Central Intelligence Agency

Political party: Republican

Term of office: January 20, 1989–January 20, 1993

Died: —

George Herbert Walker Bush, whose long record in politics and government included eight years as Ronald Reagan's vice president, was elected the 41st president in 1988. He became the first vice president since Martin Van Buren to be elected directly to the presidency.

George Bush was born in Milton, Massachusetts. He grew up with his sister and three brothers in Greenwich, Connecticut, a wealthy suburb of New York City.

At Phillips Academy in Andover, Massachusetts, where he was known as "Poppy," Bush was captain of the basketball and soccer teams, played baseball, and served as president of the senior class.

When Bush graduated from Andover in 1942, World War II was raging. Instead of going to college, Bush enlisted in the navy as a pilot.

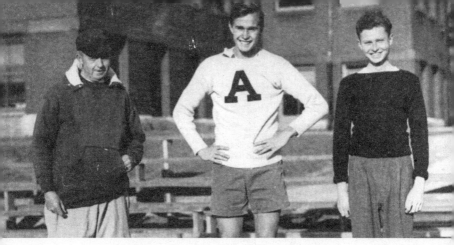

A young Bush playing soccer at Phillips Academy in Andover, Massachusetts.

HE WAS, FOR A TIME,
THE WAR'S YOUNGEST NAVY PILOT.

After the war, Bush went to college at Yale. An honors student, he graduated in 1948 with a degree in economics. He turned down an offer to join his father in a banking career in favor of starting a new life with his wife and young son in the oil fields of west Texas.

Bush's father became a U.S. senator from the state of Connecticut in 1962. Not long after, George became interested in a political career. He ran for the Senate in 1964 and lost. But the next time he ran for office, in 1966, he won a seat in the U.S. House of Representatives from the Seventh District of Texas. He served two terms.

After another unsuccessful try for the Senate, Bush was named by President Nixon to be U.S. Ambassador to the United Nations, a post he held for two years.

Bush served as chairman of the Republican National Committee during the years the Watergate scandal was breaking. After a year as U.S. envoy to China, Bush was called home to head the Central Intelligence Agency, the CIA, during troubled times there.

 155

Bush in the Oval Office.

Bush made a run for the presidency in 1980, but the Republican nomination went to Ronald Reagan. Reagan then asked Bush to run with him as his vice-presidential candidate.

As Reagan's vice president, Bush was always loyal and hard-working, supporting the president's policies even when he may not have agreed with them. Reagan showed his gratitude when Bush ran for the presidency in 1988. He not only gave Bush his endorsement but campaigned for him from one coast to the other.

In Bush's first years in office, he benefited from a solid economy and the collapse of Communism in Eastern Europe. His popularity soared to even greater heights after he sent U.S. forces to the Persian Gulf in 1990 following Iraq's invasion of Kuwait. Allied forces quickly retook Kuwait early in 1991.

Bush was much less successful at home. He promised he would not ask for new taxes—and he did. The economy slumped. Social problems got worse. Criticized for his caution and lack of leadership, Bush failed to rally the support of the American people and lost his bid for reelection in 1992.

After leaving office, Bush and his wife, Barbara, built a retirement home in Houston, Texas. In 2000, they became the longest-married presidential couple in history, surpassing the record of John and Abigail Adams, who were married for 54 years. The former president remained interested in politics, and two of his sons launched political careers of their own.

As the elder Bush approached his 90th birthday, he enjoyed reasonably good health, and still took part in his favorite sport—skydiving.

GEORGE H. W. BUSH
Important Events

1989 – In the largest oil spill in U.S. history, the oil tanker *Exxon Valdez* struck a reef and dumped nearly eleven million gallons of oil into Prince William Sound in Alaska, devastating wildlife and fouling more than 1,000 miles of coastline

1989 – East Germany opened the Berlin Wall, which had separated East and West Germany since 1961

1991 – In "Operation Desert Storm," U.S. and allied troops attacked and defeated Iraq to liberate Kuwait, which Iraq had seized in 1990

1991 – The Soviet Union disbanded, ending the Cold War

1992 – Rioters torched and looted South-Central Los Angeles after a jury cleared four policemen on all but one count in the beating of a black man

WILLIAM (BILL) JEFFERSON CLINTON

42nd President

Born: August 19, 1946

Birthplace: Hope, Arkansas

Previous experience: Lawyer, law school professor, state attorney general, governor

Political party: Democrat

Term of office: January 20, 1993– January 20, 2001

Died: —

The last American president of the twentieth century, Bill Clinton led the nation during a long stretch of full employment and economic prosperity. These factors, along with his charm and great political skills, helped Clinton enjoy lofty popularity ratings throughout most of his two presidential terms.

Clinton maintained his appeal despite many attacks on his character and a scandal that resulted in his impeachment. The president was put on trial and faced the possibility of being removed from office. Only once before, in the case of Andrew Johnson in 1868, had a president been accused of misconduct. Like Johnson, Clinton was found not guilty and remained in office.

Bill Clinton was born in Hope, Arkansas, in the southwest corner of the state. His father died in an automobile accident before his birth. When Bill was four, his mother married Roger Clinton, who legally adopted him.

In Hot Springs, Arkansas, where Bill attended public schools, he got excellent grades. He joined the Boy Scouts, helped raise money for charities, and played the saxophone in the high school band.

By the time he was 16, he was thinking of going into politics.

"I WAS GENUINELY INTERESTED IN PEOPLE AND SOLVING PROBLEMS," HE ONCE SAID. "IT WAS SOMETHING I WAS GOOD AT."

After meeting President John F. Kennedy, his idol, in Washington, DC, Clinton returned to the nation's capital to attend Georgetown University. He earned a degree in international affairs from Georgetown in 1968. He then attended Oxford University in England as a scholarship student.

Bill Clinton playing the saxophone at his inauguration.

President Clinton with his wife, Hillary Rodham Clinton and daughter, Chelsea.

Returning to the United States, he graduated from Yale Law School in 1973. After law school, Clinton taught at the University of Arkansas Law School. Meanwhile, Clinton had gotten deeply involved in politics. When Democrat George McGovern ran for president in 1972, Clinton directed his campaign in Texas. (McGovern was defeated by Richard Nixon.)

Clinton entered the political world himself in 1974 at the age of 28, attempting to win election to the House of Representatives. He lost in a close race.

Hillary Rodham, whom Clinton had met at Yale, helped during the campaign. The two were married in 1975. Their daughter, Chelsea, was born in 1980.

In 1976 Clinton was elected attorney general of the state of Arkansas. Two years later, he was elected governor for the first time. When he sought reelection in 1980, he was defeated. An unpopular license fee on new cars angered many voters. The federal government's decision to house some 18,000 Cuban refugees in Arkansas also proved damaging. When refugees at Ft. Chaffee rioted, local citizens expressed their outrage by voting against Clinton.

In 1982 Clinton ran for reelection again. He said that he had learned from past mistakes. This time he was successful. Clinton went on to serve a total of five terms as governor of Arkansas.

In the contest for the White House in 1991, Clinton and his running mate Al Gore, a Tennessee senator, defeated George H. W. Bush, the incumbent president. Texas billionaire H. Ross Perot ran as an independent candidate.

In his first term, Clinton was successful in getting legislation passed that provided tax cuts for the poor. He backed the Brady Bill, which required a waiting period for gun purchases. He supported the Family and Medical Leave Act, which protected the jobs of workers who took care of sick loved ones.

And Clinton pushed through trade agreements with Mexico and other countries.

Clinton and Gore were reelected in 1996, running against Republicans Bob Dole and Jack Kemp.

SCANDAL, COVER-UPS, AND CRIMINAL INVESTIGATIONS MARRED CLINTON'S SECOND TERM.

The most serious charge accused Clinton of an inappropriate relationship with a young woman who worked at the White House. At first, Clinton denied the relationship. He later confessed to it and apologized to the public for misleading them. The investigation of the affair led to his impeachment.

During his second term, Clinton placed more of an emphasis on foreign policy. He helped to force the withdrawal of Serb forces from Kosovo following ten weeks of NATO (the North Atlantic Treaty Organization) bombing, which was led by the United States. He pushed for trade agreements with Mexico and China.

When Clinton left office in 2001, he enjoyed one of the highest approval ratings of any U.S. president since World War II. He continued to be active in the political world: He gave speeches, helped raise money for Democrat office seekers, and carried out a number of diplomatic assignments.

Clinton continued his work with the William J. Clinton Foundation (now called the Bill, Hillary & Chelsea Clinton Foundation). Supported by donations from governments, the Foundation's efforts have been directed toward global health, the reduction of poverty, and the ending of religious and ethnic conflicts.

In 2004, Clinton's autobiography, titled *My Life*, was published. A second Clinton book, *Giving: How Each of Us Can Change the World*, was released in 2007. Both books were best sellers.

During the Democratic presidential primary campaign in 2008, when Hillary Clinton sought to be the party's nominee, Clinton enthusiastically backed his wife with speeches and fundraising efforts. But when that nomination went to Barack Obama, Clinton strongly supported him.

In 2016, Hillary Clinton sought the Democratic presidential nomination a second time. Again, her husband actively supported her, but as some observers noted, Clinton, at 69, was not as fiery as he once was. "He's more low key than he used to be," said one. That didn't seem to matter, as Mrs. Clinton still became the Democratic nominee.

WILLIAM (BILL) CLINTON
Important Events

1994 – U.S. troops entered Haiti to enforce the return of President Jean-Bertrand Aristide

1994 – In Congressional elections, Republicans took over the House of Representatives and Senate for the first time in 40 years

1995 – A terrorist bombing of the federal building in Oklahoma City killed 169 people. Timothy J. McVeigh, a U.S. Army veteran, was later convicted and sentenced to death for the bombing.

1996 – Congress passed and Clinton signed legislation that overhauled the nation's welfare system

1997 – For the first time since 1976, an American spacecraft landed on Mars

1998 – President Clinton was impeached by the House of Representatives for giving false and misleading testimony to a grand jury and for the obstruction of justice. Clinton's trial in the Senate ended in his acquittal.

1999 – NATO (the North Atlantic Treaty Organization) launched air strikes against Yugoslavia

1999 – Two teenage boys fatally shot 12 students and a teacher at Columbine High School in Littleton, Colorado

GEORGE WALKER BUSH

43rd President

Born: July 6, 1946

Birthplace: New Haven, Connecticut

Previous experience: Energy company executive, baseball club executive, governor

Political party: Republican

Term of office: January 20, 2001– January 20, 2009

Died: —

George W. Bush became the 43rd president of the United States in January 2001, following an election that was one of the most bitterly contested in more than a century. Bush's victory was notable, too, because it marked the second time in history that the son of a president was elected president. (Bush's father was George Herbert Walker Bush, the 41st president.) John Adams and John Quincy Adams were the only other father and son to claim the presidency.

In his presidential election campaign, Bush described himself as a "compassionate conservative." He said he favored limited government, personal responsibility, and strong families. He called for big tax cuts and reforms in education.

But before Bush had completed his first year in office, an event occurred that thrust these and other issues into the background. On September 11, 2001, radical Muslim hijackers slammed passenger jetliners into the twin towers of the New York World Trade Center

 164

and crashed a third jet into the Pentagon in Washington, DC. A fourth hijacked plane crashed into a field in rural Pennsylvania. Almost 3,000 people died in these attacks.

"We're at war," Bush declared a few days after.

"THERE'S BEEN AN ACT OF WAR DECLARED AGAINST AMERICA, AND WE WILL RESPOND ACCORDINGLY."

That war was to shape the Bush presidency and have a deep and long-lasting impact on the nation.

George Walker Bush was born in Connecticut, where the Bush family had its roots. His grandfather was Prescott Bush, a two-term U.S. senator from Connecticut. George's father had won distinction as a combat pilot in World War II. After the war, he was attending Yale University in New Haven when George was born.

When George was two years old, the family left Connecticut for west Texas. There the Bushes prospered in the oil business.

After the Bush family moved to Houston in 1958, George played Little League baseball and attended private school. He later enrolled

George Bush and his father, former president George Herbert Walker Bush.

at Phillips Academy in Andover, Massachusetts, the same prep school his father attended twenty years before.

After Andover, George went to Yale. An average student, he graduated in 1968. At the time, the nation was deeply involved in the Vietnam War. Antiwar demonstrations were reaching their peak. At a time when many of his generation were assigned tours of duty in Vietnam, Bush joined the Texas Air National Guard.

In 1975, after earning a master's degree from Harvard Business School, Bush went into the oil-drilling business in Midland, Texas. He launched a career in politics in 1977, running for a seat in the U.S. House of Representatives. He lost by a narrow margin.

Also in 1977, he married Laura Welch, a Midland, Texas, school librarian. They became the parents of twin girls, Barbara and Jenna.

When his father sought the presidency in 1988, Bush served as a campaign aide. After his father's election victory, Bush tried a new business venture. A serious baseball fan, he formed a group of investors that brought the Texas Rangers to Dallas.

Bush tried politics again in 1993. He announced he would be a candidate for governor of Texas. He started out as the underdog but ended up the voters' choice. As governor, Bush impressed people with his willingness to compromise and his ability to get things done. He was reelected in 1998 and his popularity grew.

Some people were now urging Bush to seek the Republican nomination for president. He assented. In the nomination sweepstakes early in 2000, Bush quickly marched to victory, brushing aside a challenge from Senator John McCain of Arizona. He then defeated Democrat Al Gore in the presidential election, one of the closest in the nation's history.

BUSH'S EARLY MONTHS AS PRESIDENT WERE SMOOTH AND PRODUCTIVE— UNTIL THE ATTACKS OF SEPTEMBER II, 2001.

In an appearance before Congress, Bush named a worldwide terrorist network known as Al Qaeda as those responsible.

As part of his global "War on Terror," Bush ordered an invasion of Afghanistan to kill or capture Al Qaeda's leaders. Before the end of 2001, Secretary of State Colin Powell announced, "We've destroyed Al Qaeda in Afghanistan."

Three days after the horrific events of September 11, 2001, President Bush visited the site of the World Trade Center, known as "Ground Zero." Here, he is shown comforting a firefighter who had lost his brother, also a firefighter, in the aftermath of the attacks.

The nation of Iraq, where President Saddam Hussein held power, was Bush's next target.

Beginning on March 20, 2003, U.S. and British forces that had been stationed in Kuwait, Iraq's neighbor to the south, invaded Iraq.

But Bush's claim of success came much too soon. Hostilities in Iraq continued. By May 2004, terrorists had killed twice as many Americans as had died in the war. Thousands of Iraqis had also died. Looting and lawlessness had caused billions of dollars in damage. As the violence continued, some said that the nation of Iraq had toppled into a full-scale civil war between religious sects.

Most Americans had backed President Bush in his decision to go to war in Iraq. But with the continued violence and terrible loss of lives, support for the president began to wane.

Nevertheless, in his bid for reelection in the fall of 2004, enough Americans continued to approve of the way the president was handling his job to provide him with a victory over his Democrat opponent, Senator John F. Kerry of Massachusetts.

Bush set out in his second term to reform Social Security and bring about important changes in the federal tax system. Possible amnesty for the millions of illegal aliens living in the United States was another of his objectives. But Bush and Congress were distracted by the war in Iraq that showed no signs of ending. At the same time, the economy looked to be sliding toward a recession. As a result, Bush was never able to realize his major goals.

During his final years in office, Bush was often the target of sharp criticism. The war in Iraq did not go well, and Bush's detractors found fault with his handling of the conflict. Severe economic problems in banking and housing led to widespread unemployment. Bush's popularity nosedived. He remained hopeful, however, that history would cast him in a favorable light.

President Bush and his wife, Laura Bush.

After leaving office in early 2009 following the inauguration of Barack Obama, Bush and his wife, Laura, settled in a suburb of Dallas, Texas. The former president busied himself with the founding and construction of the George W. Bush Library and Museum. Located on the campus of Southern Methodist University in Dallas, it opened in 2013.

Another of Bush's projects was the writing and publication of *Decision Points*, a memoir. He later wrote a biography of the elder Bush titled *41: A Portrait of My Father*.

Bush has also had to cope with health problems. During a routine examination, a blockage, which could have caused a heart attack, was discovered in one of his arteries. He underwent surgery to correct the problem.

Throughout his retirement, Bush has rarely gotten involved in presidential politics. He did, however, take the stage in Charleston, South Carolina, in February 2016 to speak on behalf of his brother Jeb who was aiming to become the Republican nominee for president, an effort that was ultimately unsuccessful.

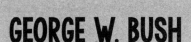

GEORGE W. BUSH
Important Events

2001 – Islamic terrorists crashed jetliners into the twin towers of the World Trade Center in New York City and the Pentagon outside Washington, DC. A fourth hijacked plane crashed in Pennsylvania. Approximately 3,000 people died in the attacks.

2001 – Congress passed and President Bush signed the Homeland Security Bill, creating a new cabinet position to coordinate anti-terrorism activity in the United States

2003 – The space shuttle *Columbia* broke apart upon reentering the earth's atmosphere, killing the seven astronauts aboard

2003 – An invasion of Iraq led by U.S. and British troops brought an end to the regime of Saddam Hussein

2003 – In what was North America's biggest blackout, some 50 million people lost electricity in eight northeastern and Mideast states and the Canadian province of Ontario

2003 – Army assault troops and special operations forces captured Iraqi leader Saddam Hussein

2004 – In one of history's worst disasters, more than 150,000 people died when a powerful earthquake in the Indian Ocean sent towering waves, called tsunamis, onto the shores of several Asian and African countries

2005 – First Democratic election in Iraq in more than 50 years

2006 – Named Katrina, the deadliest hurricane to hit the U.S. in more than 75 years struck the Gulf Coast, killing more than 1,800 people, devastating Gulfport and Biloxi, Mississippi, flooding Mobile, Alabama, and causing severe loss of life and vast property damage in New Orleans

2006 – According to the Census Bureau, the population of the United States reached 300 million

---

FUN FACT:

GEORGE W. BUSH WAS THE FIRST PRESIDENT TO RUN A MARATHON. HE TRAVELED THE 26-MILE, 385-YARD COURSE IN 3 HOURS, 44 MINUTES, AND 52 SECONDS.

BARACK OBAMA

44th President

Born: August 4, 1961

Birthplace: Honolulu, Hawaii

Previous experience: Lawyer, senator

Political party: Democrat

Term of office: January 20, 2009–January 20, 2017

Died: —

Barack Obama, a then 47-year-old senator from Illinois, shattered more than 200 years of American history on the night of November 4, 2008, by being elected the first African American president of the United States. That night, nearly a quarter of a million people crowded into Chicago's Grant Park; hundreds of thousands more watched on a huge television screen outside the park as Obama spoke, and millions of Americans watched on TV from home.

"If there is anyone out there who doubts that America is a place where anything is possible, who still wonders if the dream of our founders is alive in our times, who still questions the power of our democracy, tonight is your answer," Obama declared.

"It's been a long time coming, but tonight, because of what we did on this day, in this election, at this defining moment, change has come to America," he told the jubilant crowd.

OBAMA HAD CAMPAIGNED AS AN AGENT OF CHANGE. "CHANGE YOU CAN BELIEVE IN," HE CALLED IT.

At the time, the nation was deeply troubled. The economy was in a state of distress. People sought to cope with high unemployment and soaring prices for food and fuel. The deadly war in Iraq was in its fifth year. The United States had been involved in military action in Afghanistan since 2001.

Americans watched and waited. They asked themselves: Could the new president solve these and other tough problems by providing the sweeping change he promised?

Barack Obama was born on August 4, 1961, in Honolulu, Hawaii. His mother was white; his father was black.

His father's name was also Barack Obama. (The name Barack means "blessed.") Obama Sr. came from a poor village in Kenya, a country on the east coast of Africa. His family belonged to the Luo tribe. As a young boy, Obama Sr. herded his father's goats and attended a local school. A good student, he won a scholarship to study in Nairobi, Kenya's capital and largest city. He went on to be chosen by Kenyan leaders to further his education in the United States at the University of Hawaii in Manoa, a Honolulu neighborhood. He was 23 when he began attending classes there.

In Russian class at the university, Obama Sr. met 18-year-old Ann Dunham, a freshman. She was from Wichita, Kansas. Her mother worked in a bank. Her father farmed and worked on oil rigs. Dunham and Obama Sr. fell in love and got married.

But the marriage did not last. When Obama was two years old, his father and mother separated. The couple divorced in 1964, and Obama's father eventually went back to Kenya. Obama remained with his mother.

 173

Obama was ten years old when he next saw his father. Obama Sr. came to Hawaii to visit and stayed for a month. Little by little, the father and son came to know each other. They went to a jazz concert and spent many afternoons reading books together. Obama Sr. visited his son's school and spoke about life in Kenya.

After that visit, Obama never saw his father again. He died in an automobile accident in 1982.

In 1967, when Obama was six, his mother married again. Her new husband, Lolo Soetoro, was Indonesian. The family moved to Jakarta, the capital city of Indonesia and one of the most densely populated cities on earth. Obama's sister, Maya, was born there.

Obama's mother was unhappy with the schools in Jakarta and felt that he was not getting a good education. When Obama was ten, she sent him back to Honolulu to live with his grandparents.

Now separated from both his mother and father, Obama became close to his grandparents. They arranged for him to attend an excellent high school, the Punahou School. Barack, or Barry, as he was known at the time, had a B average.

A young Barack Obama during his time as a student at Columbia.

He seemed happiest when he was on the basketball court. He was quick and aggressive, with a solid left-handed jump shot.

"The opportunity that Hawaii offered," he told the *Honolulu Star-Bulletin*, "to experience a variety of cultures in a climate of mutual respect became an integral part of my world view, and a basis for the values I hold most dear."

After high school, Obama moved to Los Angeles. There he studied at Occidental College for two years before transferring to Columbia University in New York City, where he majored in political science. He graduated in 1983. "I spent a lot of time in the library," he said. "I didn't socialize that much. I was like a monk."

With Columbia behind him, Obama moved to Chicago to take a job as a community organizer, working in the poor neighborhoods on the city's South Side. After three years, he entered Harvard Law School, graduating in 1991. Returning to Chicago, he accepted a position as a visiting professor at the University of Chicago Law School.

There was another reason he went back to Chicago. He had fallen in love with his future wife, a young woman named Michelle Robinson. She was a lawyer as well. The two were married in 1992.

The couple's first daughter, Malia, was born in 1998. A second daughter, Sasha, arrived in 2001.

In 1996, Obama was elected to the Illinois state senate, representing the South Side Chicago neighborhood of Hyde Park. He was to spend eight years in the state senate, earning a reputation for being practical and shrewd.

HE WAS ALSO KNOWN AS SOMEONE WHO WAS WILLING TO MAKE COMPROMISES IN ORDER TO GET THINGS DONE.

In 2000, Obama made a run for a seat in the U.S. House of Representatives — and lost. But he learned from the experience. As one observer noted, Obama was "a very apt student of his own mistakes."

Three years later, Obama was presented with an unexpected opportunity when a seat in the U.S. Senate from Illinois opened. Obama became the Democratic candidate and began campaigning throughout the state. "I did my best," he said, "to say what I thought, keep it clean, and focus on substance." As he traveled and took part in televised debates, more and more people took note of the young, attractive candidate.

Leaders of the Democratic Party were among them. They chose Obama to give the keynote address at the 2004 Democratic National Convention, held in Boston.

The speech won him national acclaim. That fall, he overwhelmed his opponent in the race for the U.S. Senate, winning 70 percent of the vote.

Obama was a highly active member of the Senate. He sought improved border security and immigration reform. Gun control, climate change, and the care of American military personnel returning from Iraq and Afghanistan were other topics in which he took special interest. He made official trips to Eastern Europe, the Middle East, and Africa.

Early in 2007, at the Old State Capitol Building in Springfield, Illinois, Obama announced his candidacy for president. In the presidential primaries the next year, Obama outdueled the heavily favored Hillary Clinton to become the choice of the Democratic National Convention. He picked Delaware senator Joe Biden as his vice-presidential running mate. The two defeated Republican nominees John McCain and Sarah Palin by a comfortable margin, capturing 365 electoral votes, compared to the 173 received by McCain and Palin. They won 52.9 percent of the popular vote.

Following his first term in office, Obama could point to several major accomplishments. He and his Democratic supporters in Congress passed historic health-care reform legislation that expanded coverage to more than 30 million Americans.

"THIS IS WHAT CHANGE LOOKS LIKE," SAID OBAMA.

Obama's economic stimulus bill brought the nation's financial system back from a state of collapse. He supervised the rescue of the American automobile industry.

In April 2011, Obama announced his intention to run for reelection. In the campaign that followed, he faced Republican Mitt Romney, a former governor of Massachusetts. Obama won the election with 51 percent of the popular vote and 332 electoral votes.

President Obama with his wife, Michelle (left) and daughters Malia (middle) and Sasha (right).

Obama in the Oval Office.

During his campaign against Romney, Obama advocated for immigration reform, stricter gun control, and raising the national minimum wage. But he was never able to achieve these goals.

Congress was part of the problem. At the beginning of Obama's second term, Republicans held control of the House of Representatives. In the 2014 election, they seized control of the Senate as well. The result was that the Republican Congress blocked much of the legislation the Democratic president favored.

Obama knew there was one thing he could do to counter the inaction of Congress. He would use executive orders to change, direct, or introduce domestic policies.

Among the more than 200 executive orders issued by President Obama, one of the more controversial was one in 2012 that halted the deportation of hundreds of illegal immigrants that were brought to the U.S. as children. Another executive order boosted the minimum wage for federal workers under contract from $7.25 to $10.10.

The way in which future historians will view Obama's presidency is likely to be based on some of the policies and programs for which he was responsible. A handful of these could be of enormous importance in the years to come.

For example, on the domestic front, Obama introduced the Affordable Care Act, also known as ObamaCare, which has led to sweeping changes in America's health care system. As of 2016, more than fifteen million people had gained coverage from ObamaCare and the expansion of the Medicare program for those with low incomes.

OBAMACARE, IN TERMS OF THE MASSIVE SOCIAL BENEFITS IT MAY ONE DAY PROVIDE, HAS BEEN COMPARED TO SOCIAL SECURITY AND MEDICARE.

In the later years of his administration, the president called for a program to combat global warming and climate change. Global warming refers to the gradual increase in the earth's surface temperature through the release of carbon dioxide and other greenhouse gases. Rising temperatures could lead to the melting of Arctic glaciers, leading to rising sea levels, and unusual and extreme weather events.

Thanks largely to President Obama's efforts, climate change negotiations in Paris in 2015 led world leaders to set ambitious goals to reduce greenhouse gas emissions. The talks leading to the agreement were only possible, the president said, "because America led with clean energy here at home and strong diplomacy around the world."

Through another of Obama's efforts, six world powers, including the United States, agreed in July 2015 to a significant nuclear deal against the nation of Iran. Said the president: "We succeeded in forging a strong deal to stop Iran from obtaining a nuclear weapon."

Obama didn't accomplish everything he wanted to in his eight years in office; he didn't expect to. But what he did achieve has led him to be rated as one of the more successful presidents of modern times.

BARACK OBAMA
Important Events

2009 – Sonia Sotomayor was sworn in by John Roberts, chief justice of the Supreme Court, to become the first Latina and third woman to join the court

2009 – Noted for his "extraordinary efforts to strengthen international diplomacy and cooperation between peoples," President Obama was awarded the Nobel Peace Prize by the Norwegian Nobel Committee

2010 – A gas explosion on an exploratory drilling platform in the Gulf of Mexico killed 11 people and ruptured pipes, causing a monstrous oil leak that lasted over four months and tragically polluted the Gulf of Mexico and coastal areas

2010 – A catastrophic earthquake struck near the Haitian capital of Port-au-Prince, bringing death to more than 220,000 people and causing more than $8 billion in destruction and damage

2010 – Congress passed and President Obama signed a comprehensive health-care law, officially known as the Patient Protection and Affordable Care Act, meant to extend health-insurance coverage to some 30 million Americans

2011 – An earthquake, described as the most powerful in recorded history, struck Japan. It triggered a devastating tsunami that brought death to over 18,000 people and caused property damage estimated at more than $235 billion.

2011 – In Abbottabad, Pakistan, a team of U.S. Navy Seals assassinated al-Qaeda leader Osama bin Laden, whose role as a terrorist leader included the attack on the World Trade Center in New York, on September 11, 2001

2011 – The war in Iraq officially ended on December 15, with a flag-lowering ceremony at U.S. headquarters in Baghdad

2015 – The Supreme Court recognized the right to same-sex marriage

2015 – Negotiations completed with Iran to prevent the production of nuclear weapons

2015 – United States resumed formal diplomatic relations with Cuba, with embassies opened in Washington D.C. and Havana

2016 – President Obama traveled to Havana for two days, becoming the first American president to visit Cuba since Calvin Coolidge in 1928

FUN FACT:
BARACK OBAMA COLLECTS *SPIDER-MAN* AND *CONAN THE BARBARIAN* COMIC BOOKS.

DONALD TRUMP

45 President

Born: June 14, 1946

Birthplace: New York, New York

Previous experience: Businessman

Political party: Republican

Term of office: January 20, 2017– January 20, 2021

Died: —

TV personality and producer. Real estate developer. Builder. Author. Casino owner. Hotelier. Team owner. Professional model manager.

Over the past few decades, Donald Trump held one or more of these positions. He had never, however, held elective office. And nothing in his lengthy professional résumé suggested that he had any experience in governing, diplomacy, or politics. So it may seem somewhat incredible that on January 20, 2017, Trump was able to add "President of the United States" to his impressive job list.

Donald Trump was born on June 14, 1946, in the borough (neighborhood) of Queens in New York City. He had two brothers, one older, one younger, and two older sisters.

The Trump family lived in a section of Queens known as Jamaica Estates, a wealthy community of stately homes on tree-lined streets.

In Trump's early years, his father, a developer and contractor, was an important influence. Trump recalled his father saying to him,

"THE MOST IMPORTANT THING IN LIFE IS TO LOVE WHAT YOU'RE DOING, BECAUSE THAT'S THE ONLY WAY YOU'LL EVER BE REALLY GOOD AT IT."

Trump admitted that when he was young he liked to stir up things. In school gatherings he was often aggressive and disruptive. He liked to test people.

After enduring years of his unruly behavior, Trump's parents decided that he could benefit from military training. When Trump was thirteen and beginning eighth grade, his parents enrolled him at the New York Military Academy, a private school for boys (and later girls) in Cornwall, NY.

The young Trump was not thrilled by his parents' decision. Students began each day at the Academy at dawn and were in bed by 10 p.m. The young men wore uniforms and took part in military drills. Besides taking standard academic subjects such as mathematics, history, and biology, Trump and his classmates also received instruction in military history and shooting.

Eventually Trump responded favorably to life with military discipline, as his parents had hoped. He worked hard and was promoted steadily in the school's version of military rankings. In his senior year, Trump was promoted to the rank of captain. He got to be a "big shot" on campus, a classmate said.

"There was an air about him," another student remembered, "as if he knew he was just there passing time until he went on to something greater."

From New York Military Academy, Trump went on to Fordham

Donald Trump and his father, Fred Trump.

University in New York. "I wanted to be close to home," he said.

Trump stayed at Fordham for only two years, moving on to the Wharton School of Finance at the University of Pennsylvania in Philadelphia. Wharton graduates are said to earn some of the highest starting salaries of any business school in the world. Trump felt that since he planned to have a business career, it was the only place to go. He graduated from Wharton in 1968 with a degree in economics.

Later in life, and when campaigning for the presidency in 2016, Trump liked to remind audiences where he went to college. "I went to the Wharton School of Business," Trump said several times during a speech in Phoenix, Arizona. "I'm, like, a really smart person."

After graduating, Trump moved back to the family home in Queens and went to work for his father in real estate development and construction. But to the younger Trump there was a kind of nastiness connected to the work. When he would accompany rent collectors on their rounds, they would sometimes encounter tenants who refused to pay what they owed. This often resulted in angry confrontations.

Besides the unpleasantness, there was the matter of profit. Trump felt the business caused you to be tightfisted, or cheap. You had to, as he put it, "pinch pennies." There was no room for luxuries.

But Trump had other ideas.

HE WANTED TO BE INVOLVED IN PROJECTS THAT REFLECTED WEALTH AND ELEGANCE.

This may have been a trait he inherited from his mother. He wrote that she loved "splendor and magnificence."

Trump had his eye on Manhattan, where big money could be made. He moved there in 1971, while continuing to work for his father in Queens. Little by little, as he walked the city, he learned more about Manhattan's real estate, the good and the bad.

When he started out on his own, Trump had no real experience in the real estate field in Manhattan. But what he lacked in experience, he made up for in energy, enthusiasm, and a willingness to take on risky projects.

Today, if you were to visit Manhattan, Trump's skill as a deal-maker is apparent everywhere. There's Trump Tower, the Fifth Avenue skyscraper just south of Central Park, where he and his family live. There's Trump Place, Trump Plaza, Trump Park, 610 Park Ave., Trump Park Avenue, and the Trump World Tower (at 72 stories, it was the tallest apartment tower in New York for many years). There's also the Trump Building at 40 Wall St. and a Trump-owned skating rink in Central Park.

Over time, Trump expanded his reach beyond New York City. His other real estate developments include, among others, the Mar-a-Lago resort in Palm Beach, Florida, which is his winter home; an office building in downtown San Francisco; a 64-story hotel and residential tower in Las Vegas; and the new Trump International Hotel in Washington, DC.

Along with his worldwide activity as a developer and builder, Trump also carved out a successful career in television, chiefly as the executive producer and host of *The Apprentice,* a television reality game show that sought to judge the business skills of contestants each week.

IT GAVE BIRTH TO A POPULAR CATCHPHRASE, "YOU'RE FIRED!" THAT TRUMP DELIVERED AT THE END OF EACH EPISODE WITH GREAT DRAMA.

For a time, *The Apprentice* ranked as one of the highest rated shows on television.

Other Trump ventures in television, in partnership with NBC, include the televising of the Miss Universe, Miss USA, and Miss Teen USA beauty pageants. There's also Trump Model Management, founded in 1999, a New York modeling agency.

At times, Trump's touch has not always been golden, and he has had his share of business setbacks. Foremost among them were four business bankruptcies, situations in which he failed to satisfy the financial claims of corporations, big banks, employees, and suppliers. The four bankruptcies involved gambling casinos in Atlantic City, New Jersey, that carried his name.

In his personal life, Trump has had three marriages, two of which ended in divorce. He has five children and eight grandchildren.

Trump married Melania Knass in 2005. Mrs. Trump was born in Yugoslavia (now Slovenia) in 1970. She began a modeling career at age 16, working in Milan and Paris. She continued to model after moving to New York in 1996. Two years later, she met Donald Trump. Their

Donald Trump in his office.

son, Barron William Trump, was born in 2006. Mrs. Trump speaks five languages—Slovenian, English, French, German, and Serbian.

While Trump had virtually no experience in politics or governing when he first began to consider a presidential bid, he was certainly not an unknown figure. His name was emblazoned on buildings across the country, and his wealth, personal life, brash manner, and willingness to express his opinion on almost any subject had made him internationally famous. He has ranked as high as number 14 on *Forbes* magazine's list of the "World's Highest-Paid Celebrities."

When the idea of running for president was suggested to him in a magazine interview from as early as 1990, Trump noted, "The working guy would elect me. He likes me. When I walk down the street, those cabbies start yelling out their windows."

In 2012, he did some minor campaigning for the Republican nomination but decided it was not to be and withdrew early from the running. He may have regretted his decision, as he later said, "I would've won the race against [President Barack] Obama. He would've been easy."

Trump's real journey to the White House began in June 2015 when he announced he was in the running to become the Republican presidential nominee.

THERE WERE 16 OTHER CANDIDATES IN THE RACE, MAKING IT THE BIGGEST PRIMARY ELECTION FOR A MAJOR POLITICAL PARTY IN AMERICA IN 100 YEARS.

Neither his rivals for the nomination nor the media took him seriously at first. Trump was said to lack experience, even temperament, and the judgment needed for the job. Many people thought that he would eventually withdraw.

Even when Trump jumped into an early lead in the primary polls, analysts said it was only because his name was so well known. It was predicted that his popularity would soon fade.

That never happened. The political outsider continued to win widespread approval with his message calling for immigration control

Donald Trump and Vice President Mike Pence.

and doing whatever was necessary to make the economy strong again. Trump soon began to be seen as a serious threat to the other candidates.

While he ran as a Republican, some media sources declared Trump to be a moderate conservative. One of his proposed plans during the campaign was to build a 1,000-mile-long wall along the Mexico-United States border to control the flow of immigrants. He also promised to put a temporary ban on non-citizen Muslims entering the United States due to what he considered to be a real threat of ISIS terrorists.

When it came to economic issues, Trump announced that he opposed cuts in Social Security and Medicare. He joined other Republican candidates in urging Congress to rid the nation of the Affordable Care Act, also known as ObamaCare.

"MAKE AMERICA GREAT AGAIN!" WAS HIS CAMPAIGN'S BATTLE CRY.

Trump appealed to a high percentage of working-class Republican voters who were fed up with the party's leadership. They liked Trump because he was confident and took firm positions. They believed he could get things done, that he could bring about change in the country. "He's saying what we feel," noted one of his supporters.

But it wasn't merely what Trump had to say that excited many voters. It also was his rough-and-tumble style of campaigning. He turned televised debates into slugfests. He called one of his opponents a "choke artist." He branded another as a "basket case" and cited him as "the single biggest liar" he ever met. He shouted at his rivals; they shouted back.

Soon, Trump and his antics were receiving near-constant daily coverage from news outlets, talk radio, and TV stations. While his opponents were spending tens of millions of dollars on TV and radio advertising, Trump was essentially getting free media coverage.

Trump won the New Hampshire Republican primary and before the end of February captured two additional state contests. His dominance continued in the months that followed.

By mid-March 2016, Trump was the clear front-runner for the Republican nomination. He captured 15 of the first 24 primaries and caucuses and accumulated far more delegates than his chief rivals, Texas senator Ted Cruz and Ohio governor John Kasich. One by one, the many other opponents dropped out of the race, with Trump eventually winning the party nomination.

Once the general election campaign got underway, Hillary Clinton was cited as the favorite by most polls. Voters knew that she had much more experience in governing than Donald Trump. But they also had negative feelings about her. They felt she wasn't quite honest, that she wasn't authentic or real. This distrust of Mrs. Clinton helped Trump to eventually come out on top in the presidential race.

WHAT ONCE MAY HAVE SEEMED BEYOND BELIEF HAD ACTUALLY HAPPENED.

"My life has been about victories. I've won a lot. I win a lot. I win—when I do something, I win. And even in sports, I always won," Trump had said early on.

During the primary campaign, Trump often spoke about winning. He promised to "win our new future struggles, which may be many, which may be complex, but we will win if I become president."

By defeating Hillary Clinton in the 2016 presidential election, Donald Trump added to his winning record, just as he had predicted. Americans hoped that as the nation's chief executive, his string of victories would continue.

President and Term	Political Party
George Washington 1789–1797	None
John Adams 1797–1801	Federalist
Thomas Jefferson 1801–1809	Democratic-Republican
James Madison 1809–1817	Democratic-Republican
James Monroe 1817–1825	Democratic-Republican
John Quincy Adams 1825–1829	Democratic-Republican
Andrew Jackson 1829–1837	Democrat
Martin Van Buren 1837–1841	Democrat
William Henry Harrison 1841	Whig
John Tyler 1841–1845	Whig
James Knox Polk 1845–1849	Democrat
Zachary Taylor 1849–1850	Whig
Millard Fillmore 1850–1853	Whig
Franklin Pierce 1853–1857	Democrat
James Buchanan 1857–1861	Democrat
Abraham Lincoln 1861–1865	Republican
Andrew Johnson 1865–1869	Democrat
Ulysses Simpson Grant 1869–1877	Republican
Rutherford Birchard Hayes 1877–1881	Republican
James Abram Garfield 1881	Republican
Chester Alan Arthur 1881–1885	Republican
Grover Cleveland 1885–1889	Democrat
Benjamin Harrison 1889–1893	Republican
Grover Cleveland 1893–1897	Democrat
William McKinley 1897–1901	Republican
Theodore (Teddy) Roosevelt 1901–1909	Republican
William Howard Taft 1909–1913	Republican

President and Term	Political Party
Woodrow Wilson 1913–1921	Democrat
Warren Gamaliel Harding 1921–1923	Republican
John Calvin Coolidge 1923–1929	Republican
Herbert Clark Hoover 1929–1933	Republican
Franklin Delano Roosevelt 1933–1945	Democrat
Harry S. Truman 1945–1953	Democrat
Dwight (Ike) David Eisenhower 1953–1961	Republican
John (Jack) Fitzgerald Kennedy 1961–1963	Democrat
Lyndon Baines Johnson 1963–1969	Democrat
Richard Milhous Nixon 1969–1974	Republican
Gerald Rudolph Ford 1974–1977	Republican
James (Jimmy) Earl Carter, Jr. 1977–1981	Democrat
Ronald Reagan 1981–1989	Republican
George Herbert Walker Bush 1989–1993	Republican
William (Bill) Jefferson Clinton 1993–2001	Democrat
George Walker Bush 2001–2009	Republican
Barack Obama 2009–2017	Democrat
Donald Trump 2017–2021	Republican

President Obama and past presidents George Walker Bush, Bill Clinton, George Herbert Walker Bush, and James Earl Carter Jr.